WELCOME KIDS COLORING BOOK

Large Size 8.5" x 11" inches
(21.59 x 27.94 cm.)

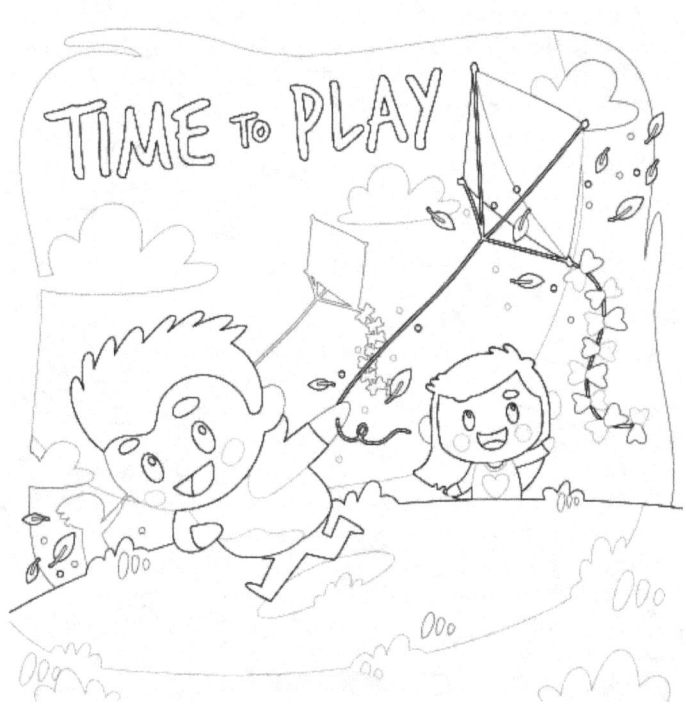

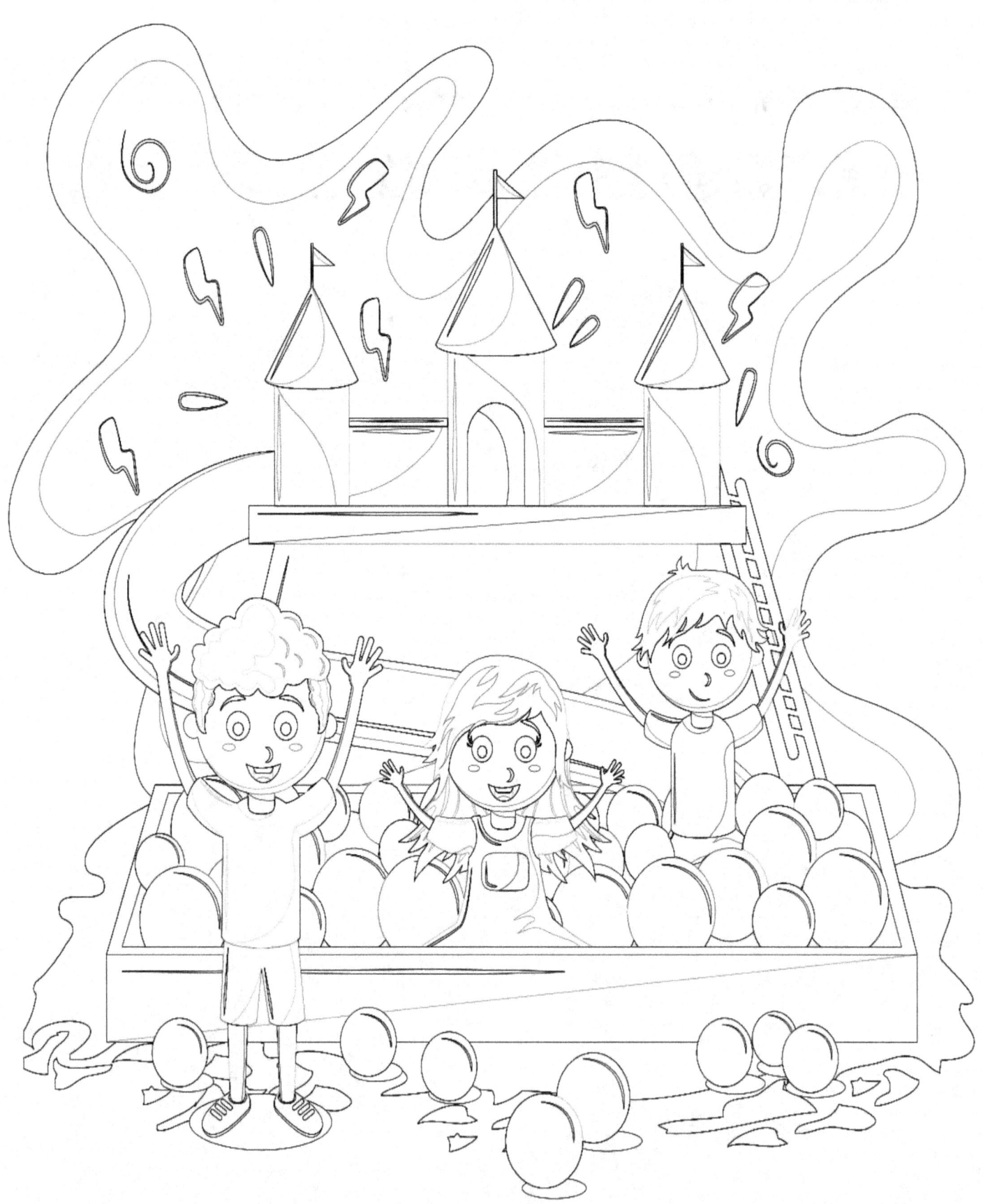

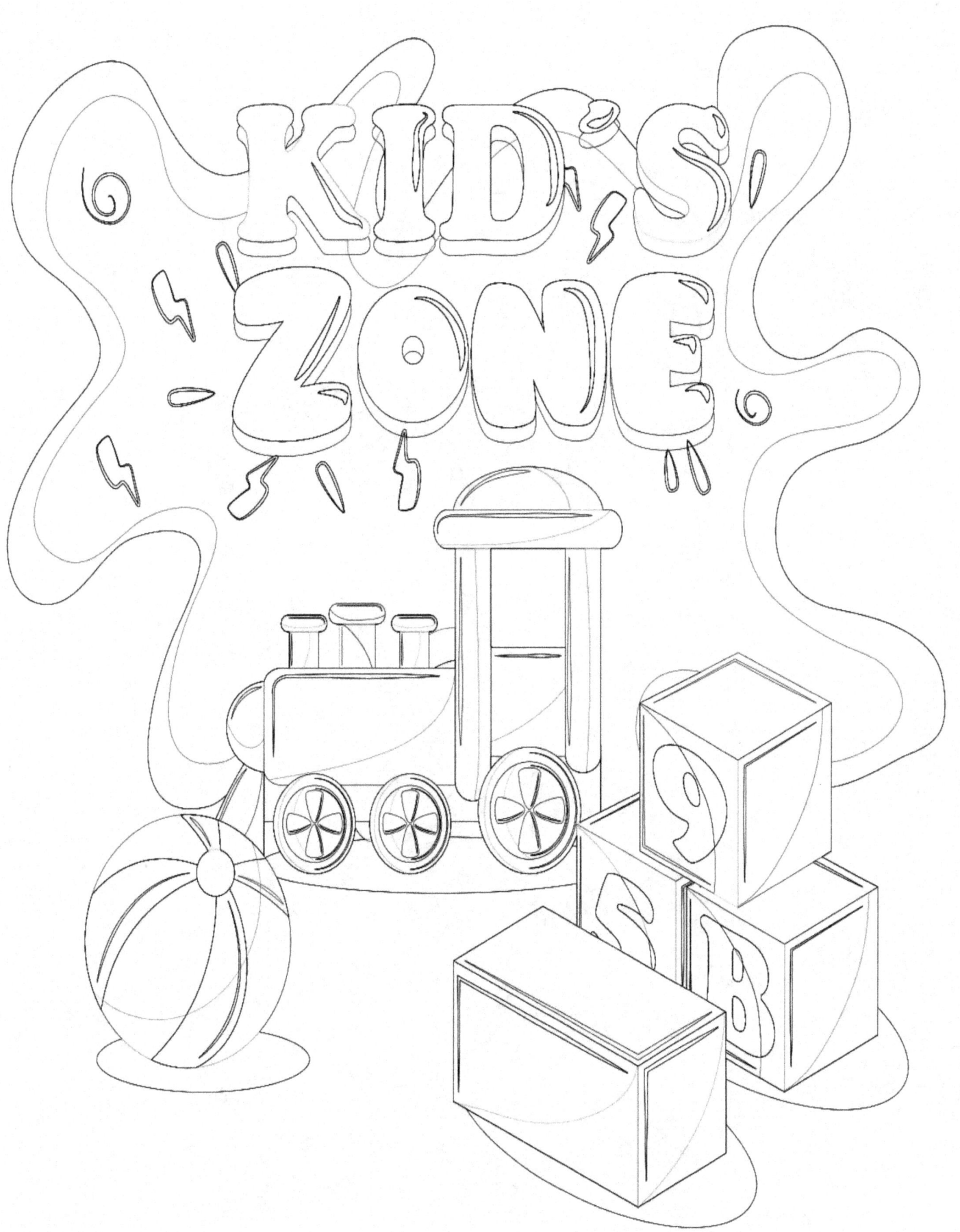

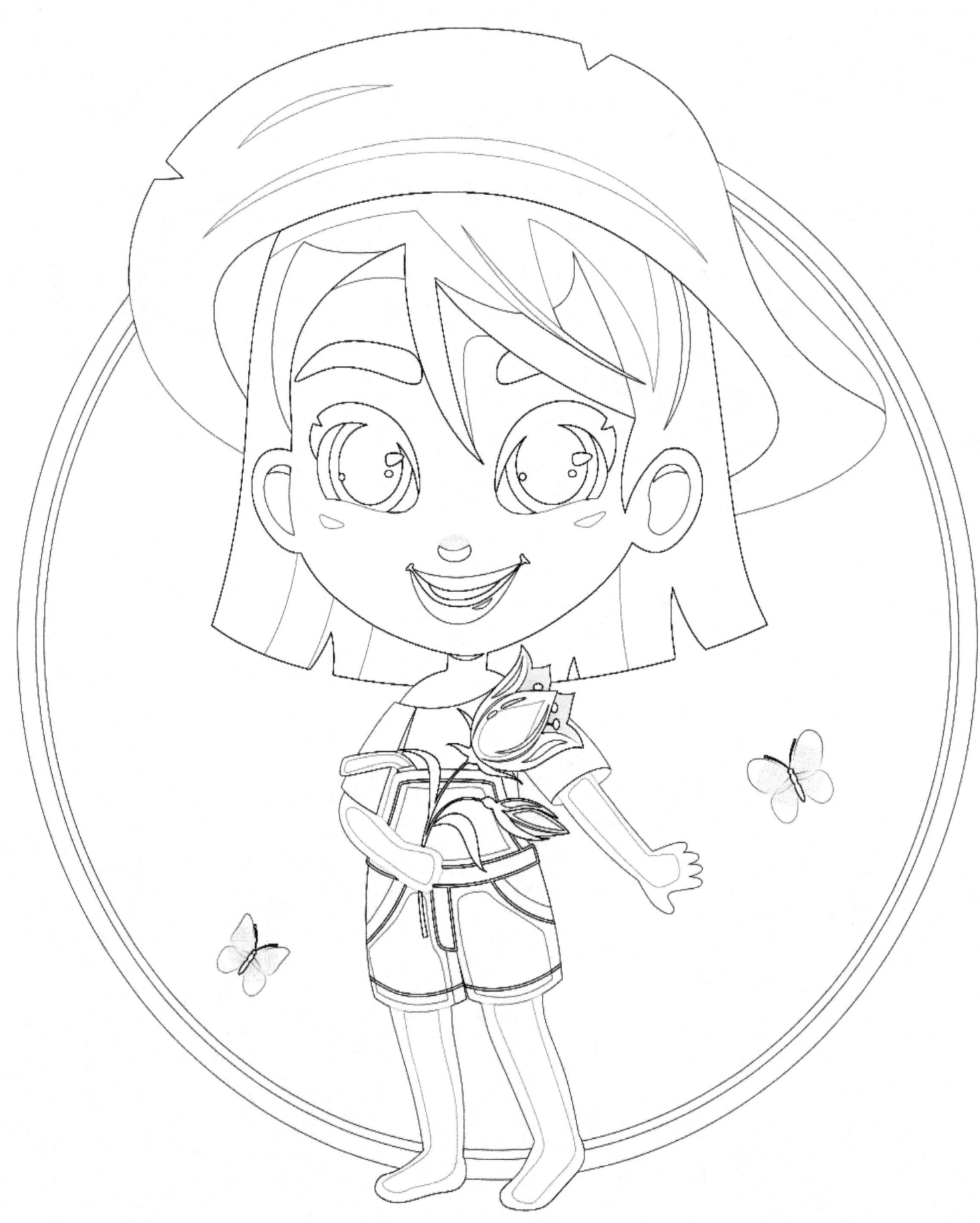

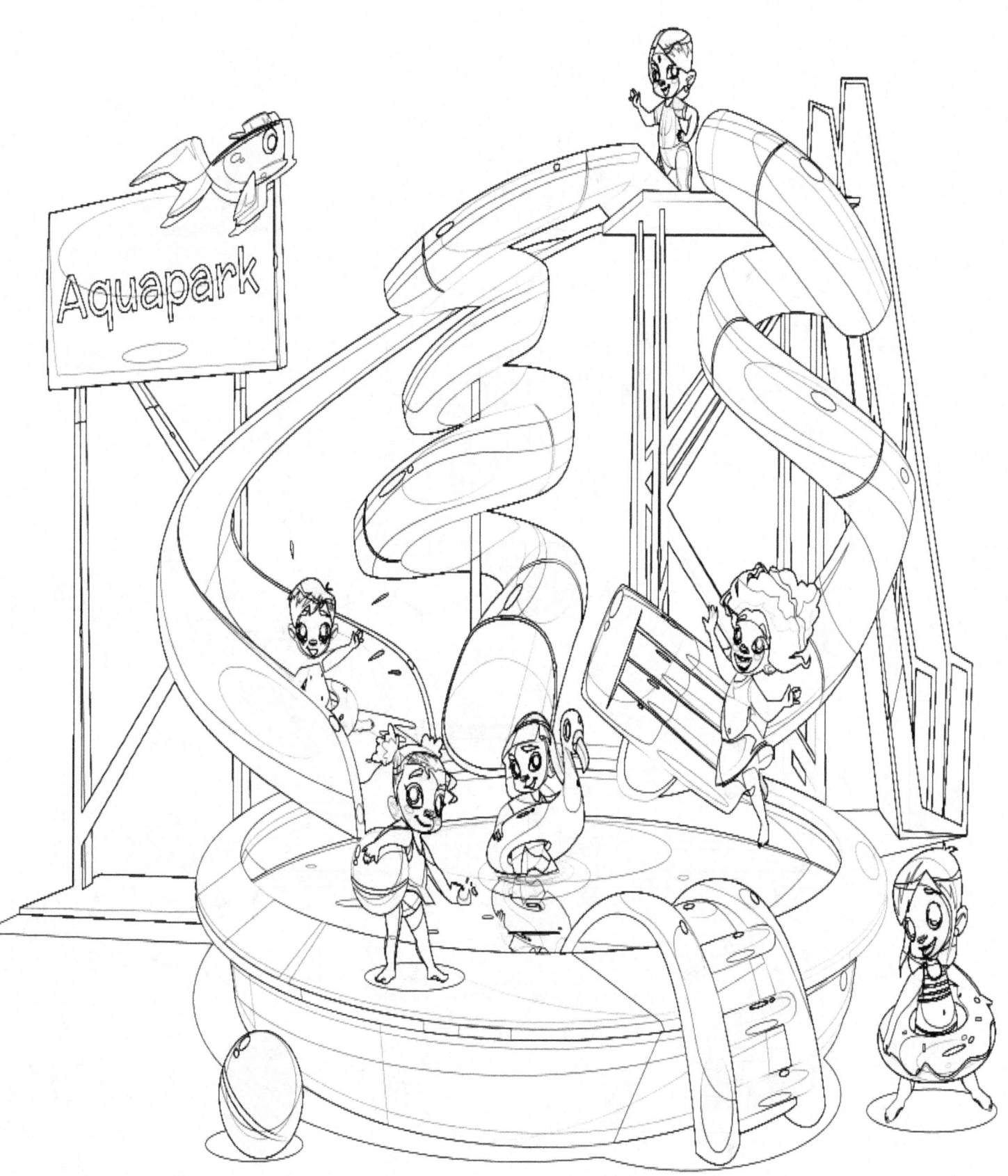

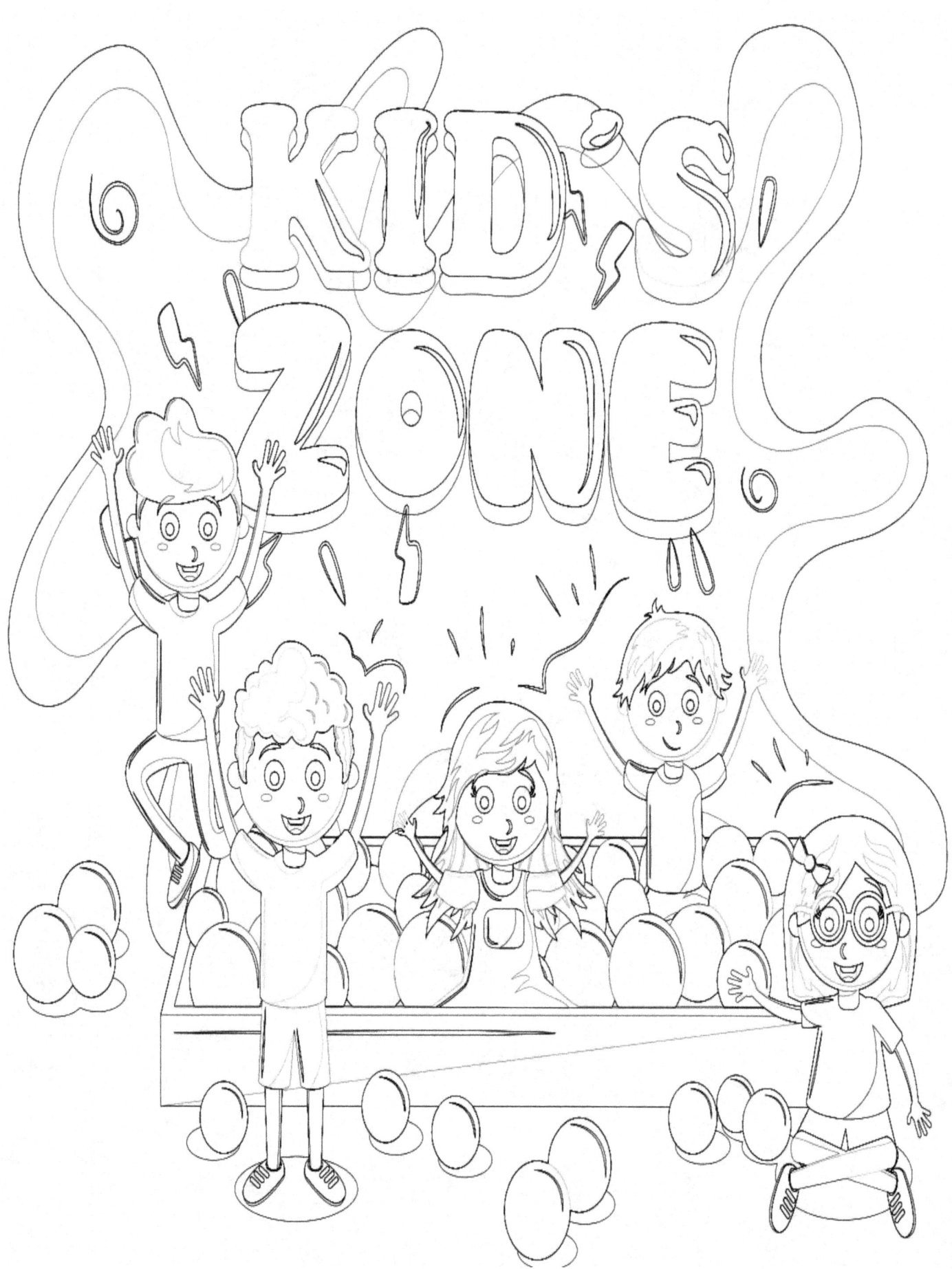

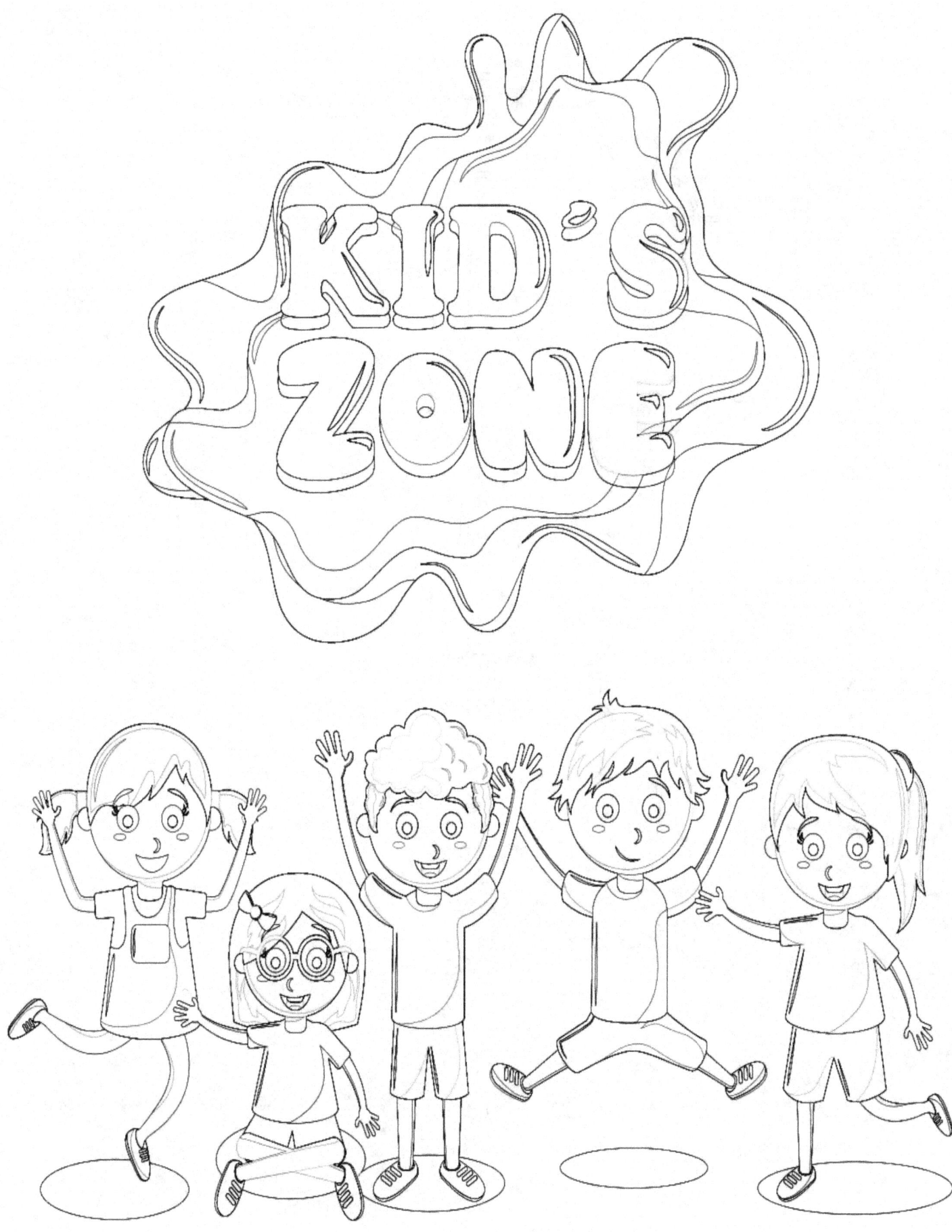

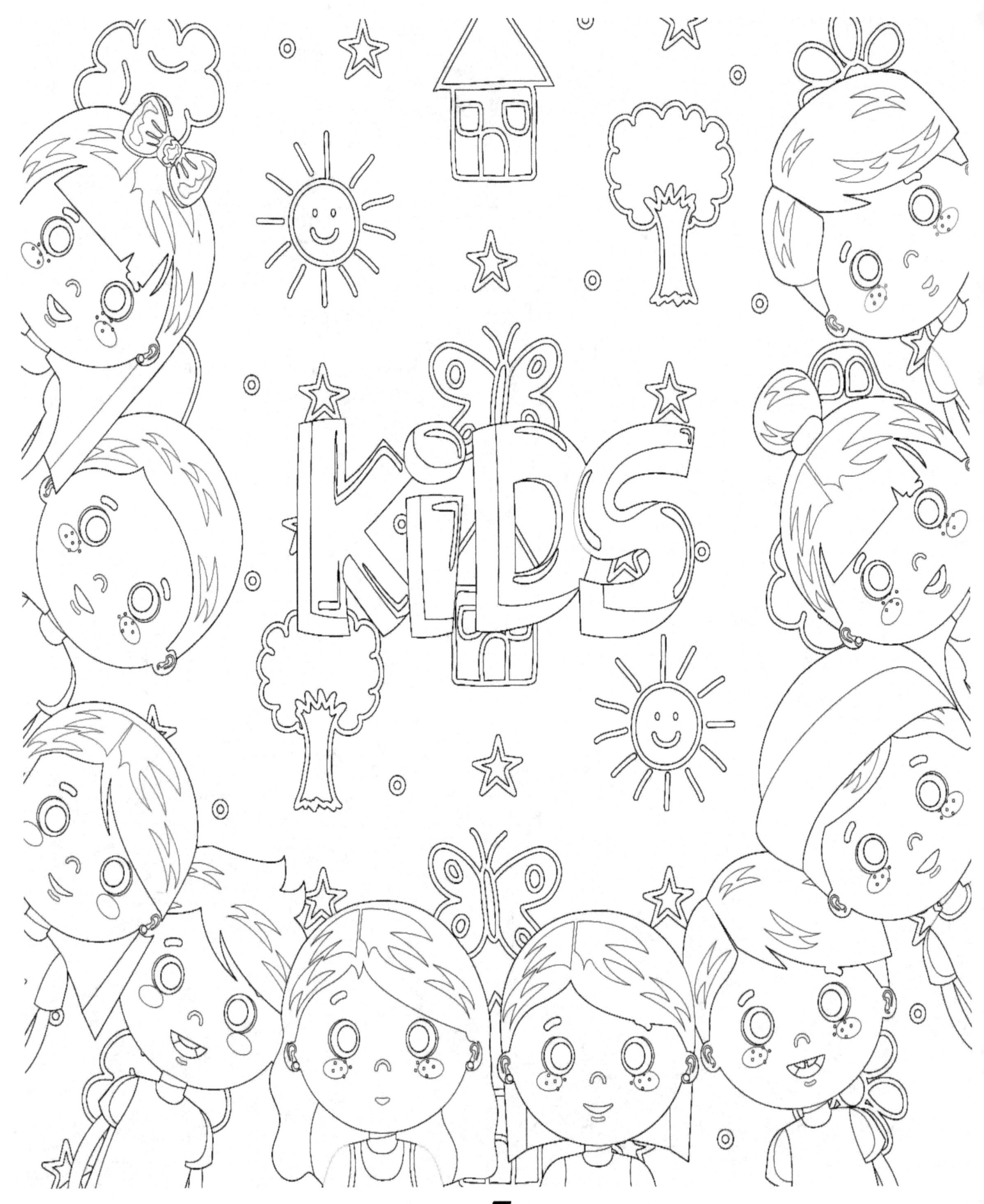

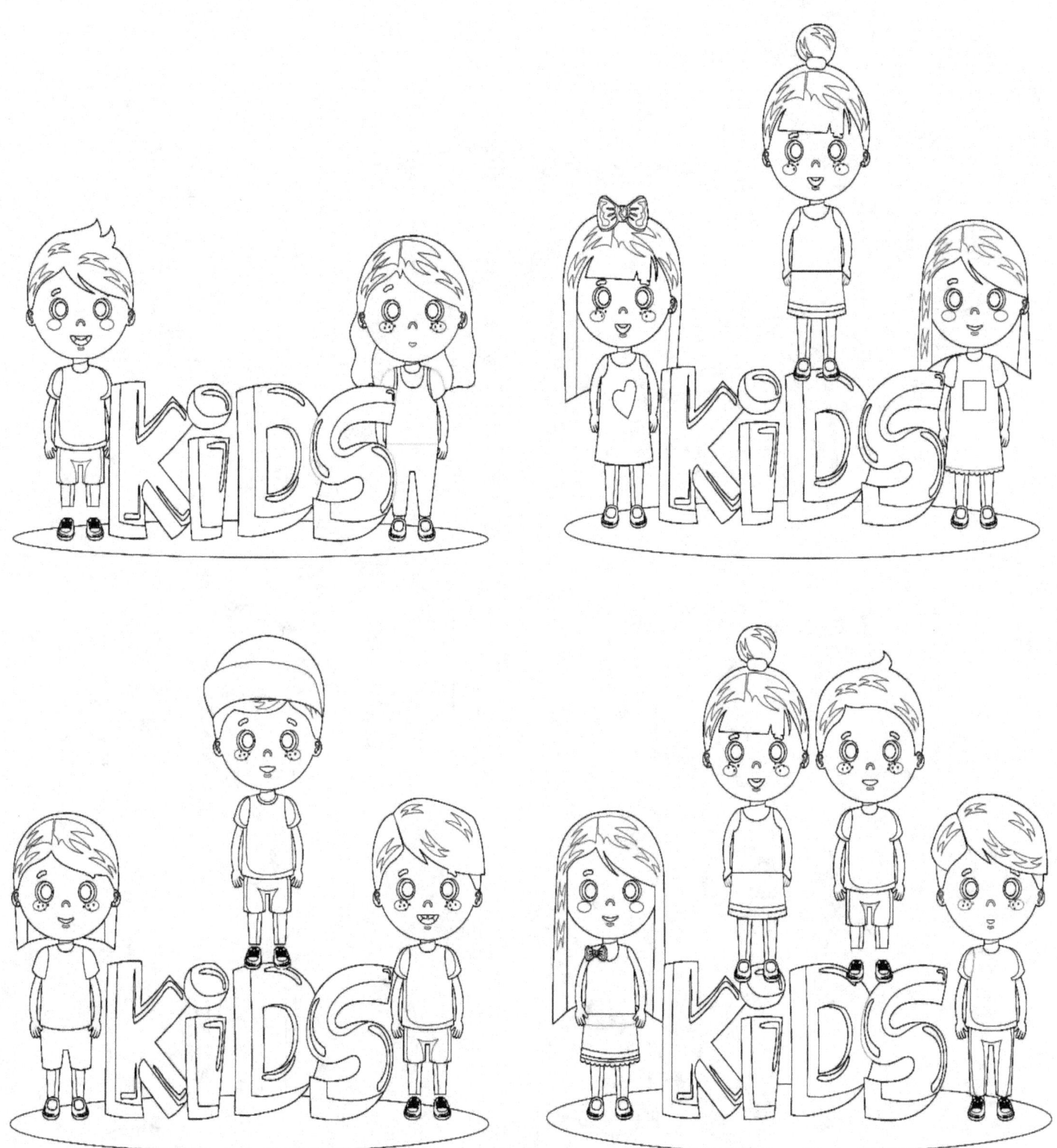

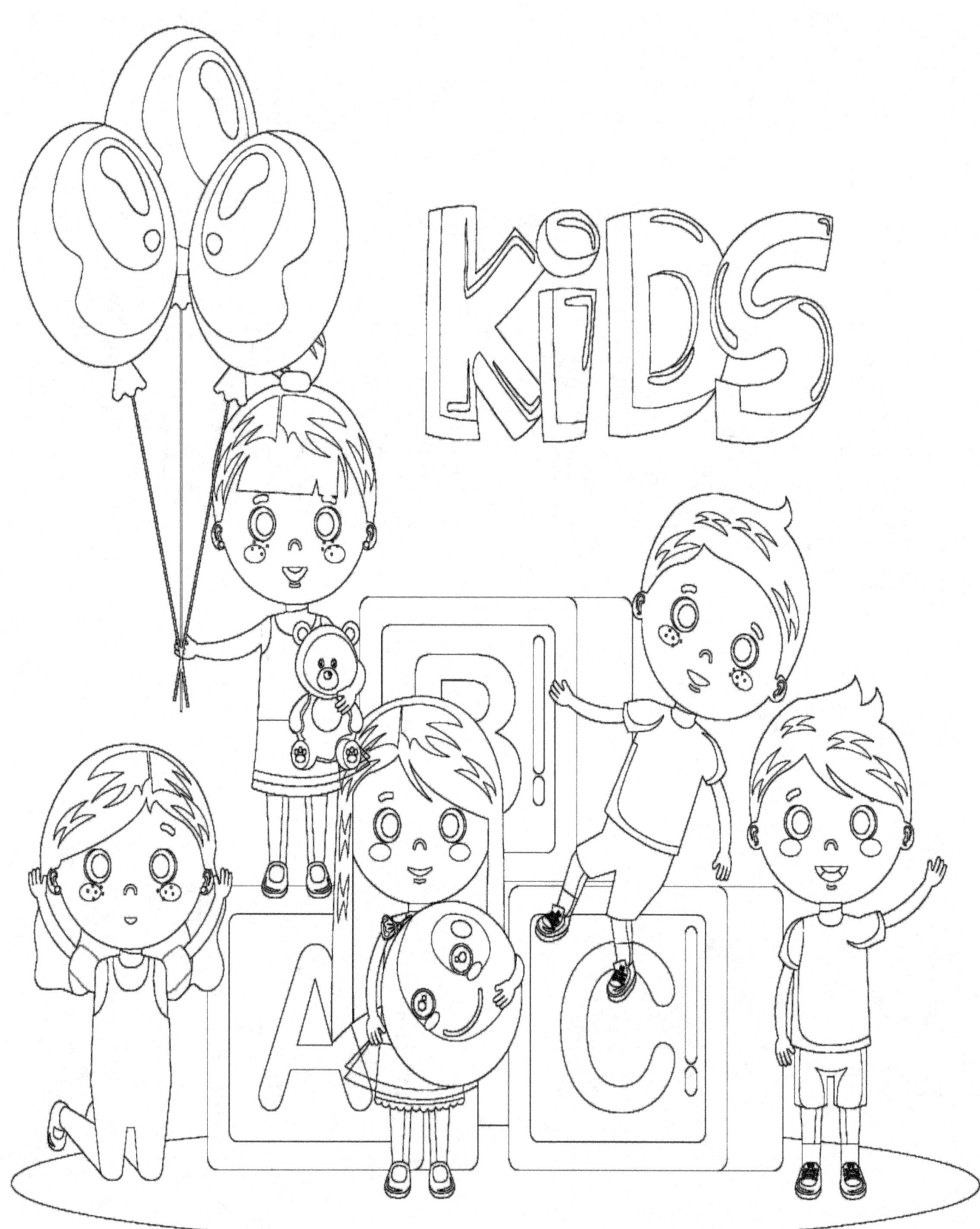

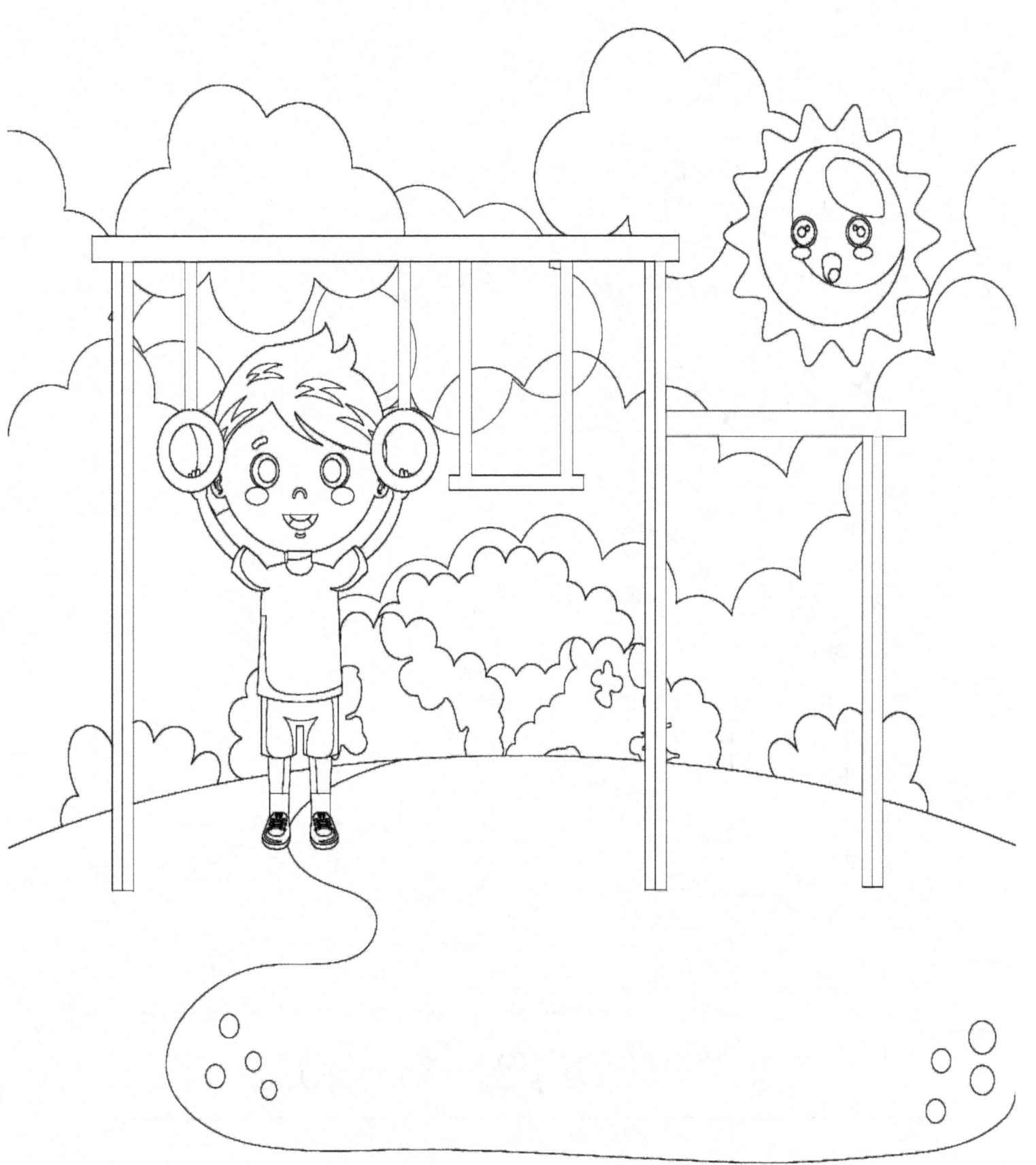

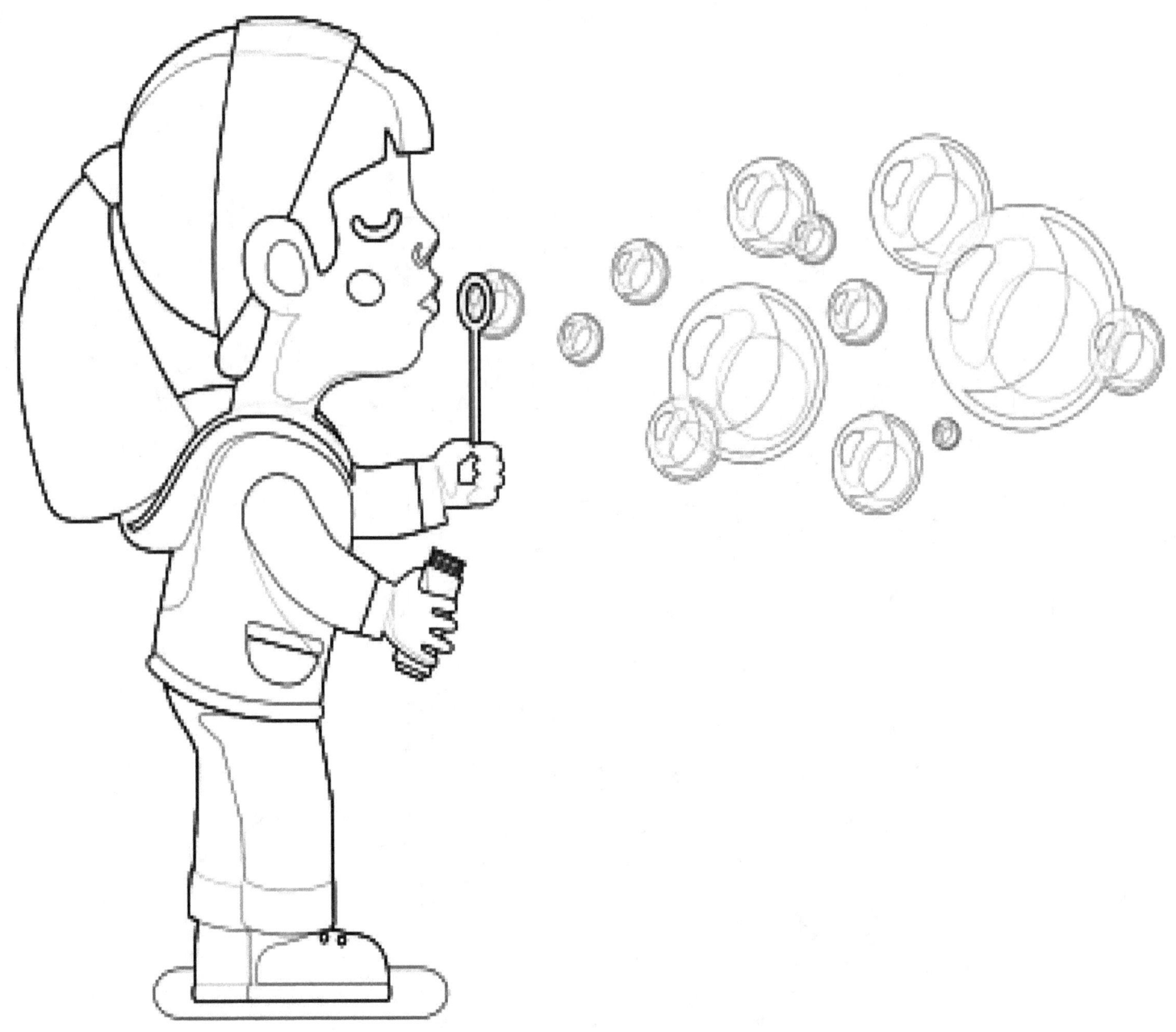

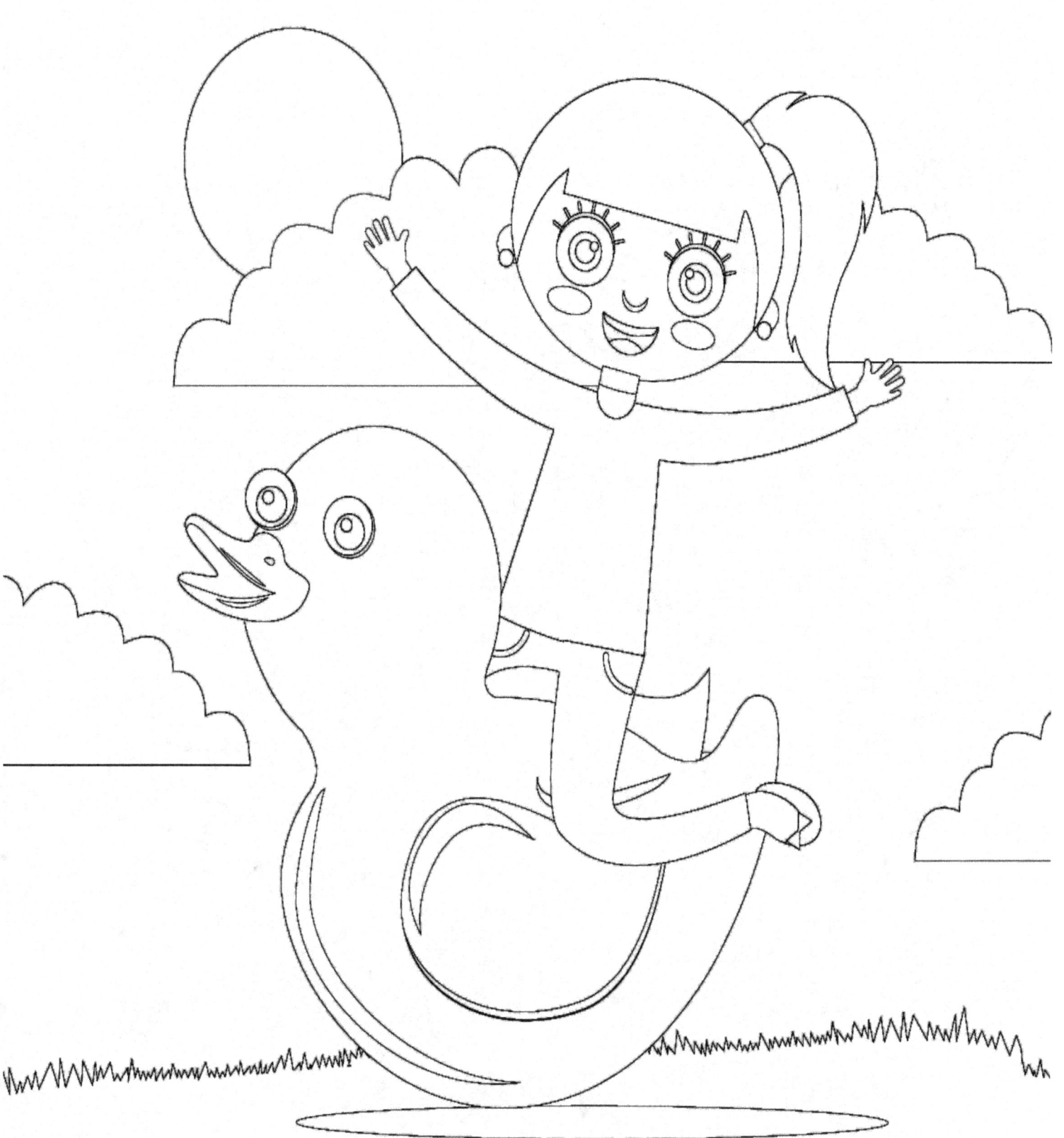

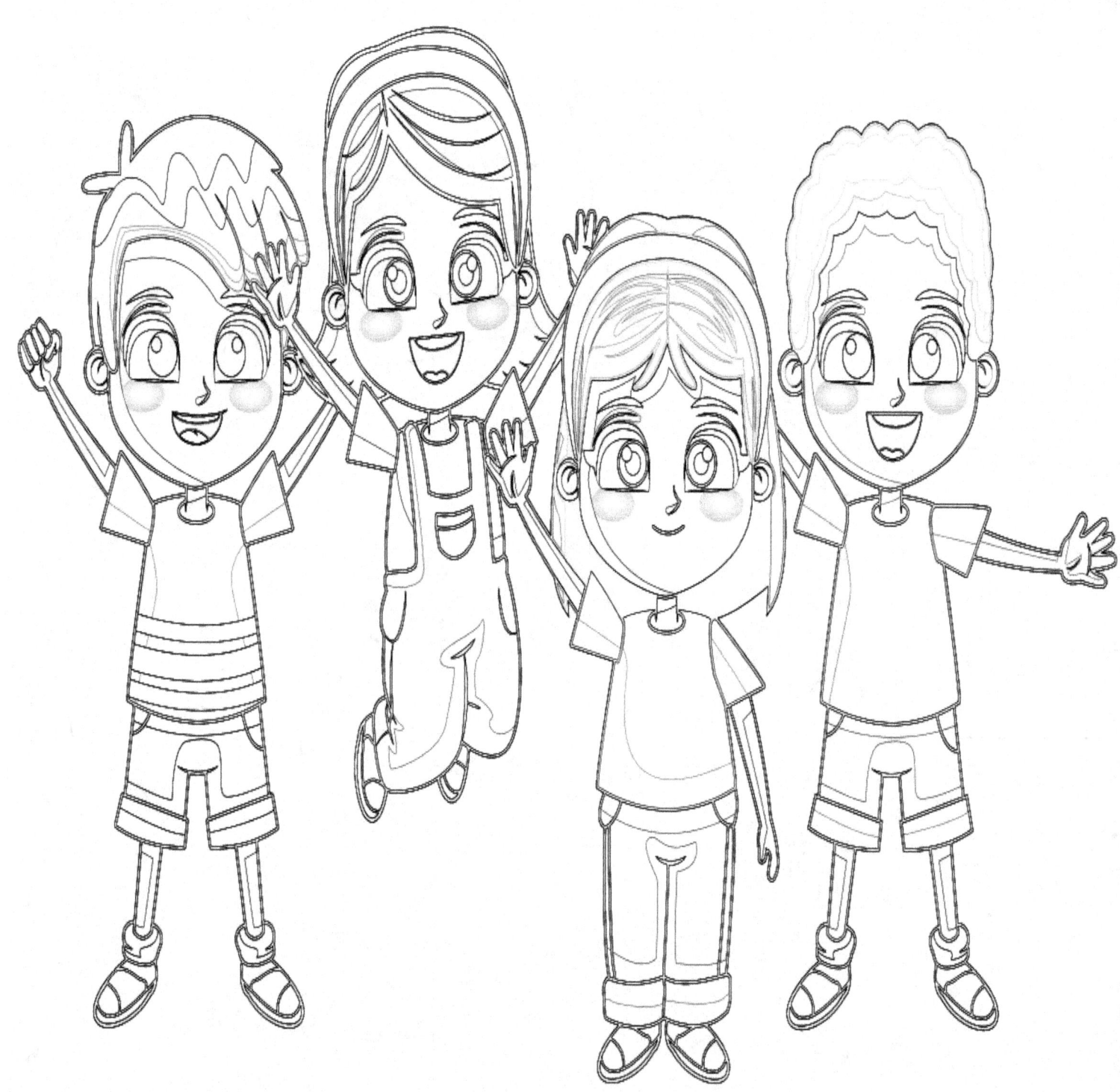

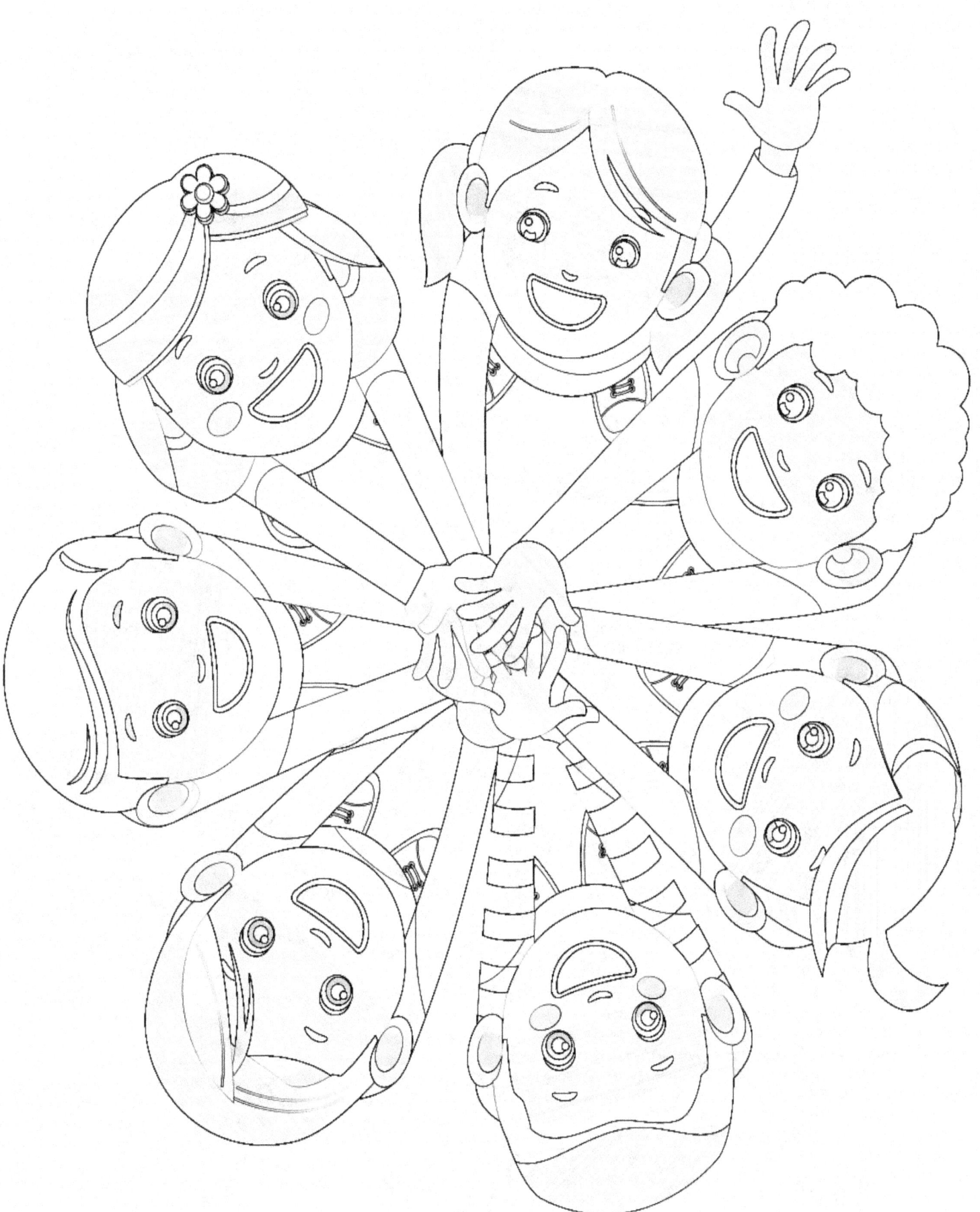

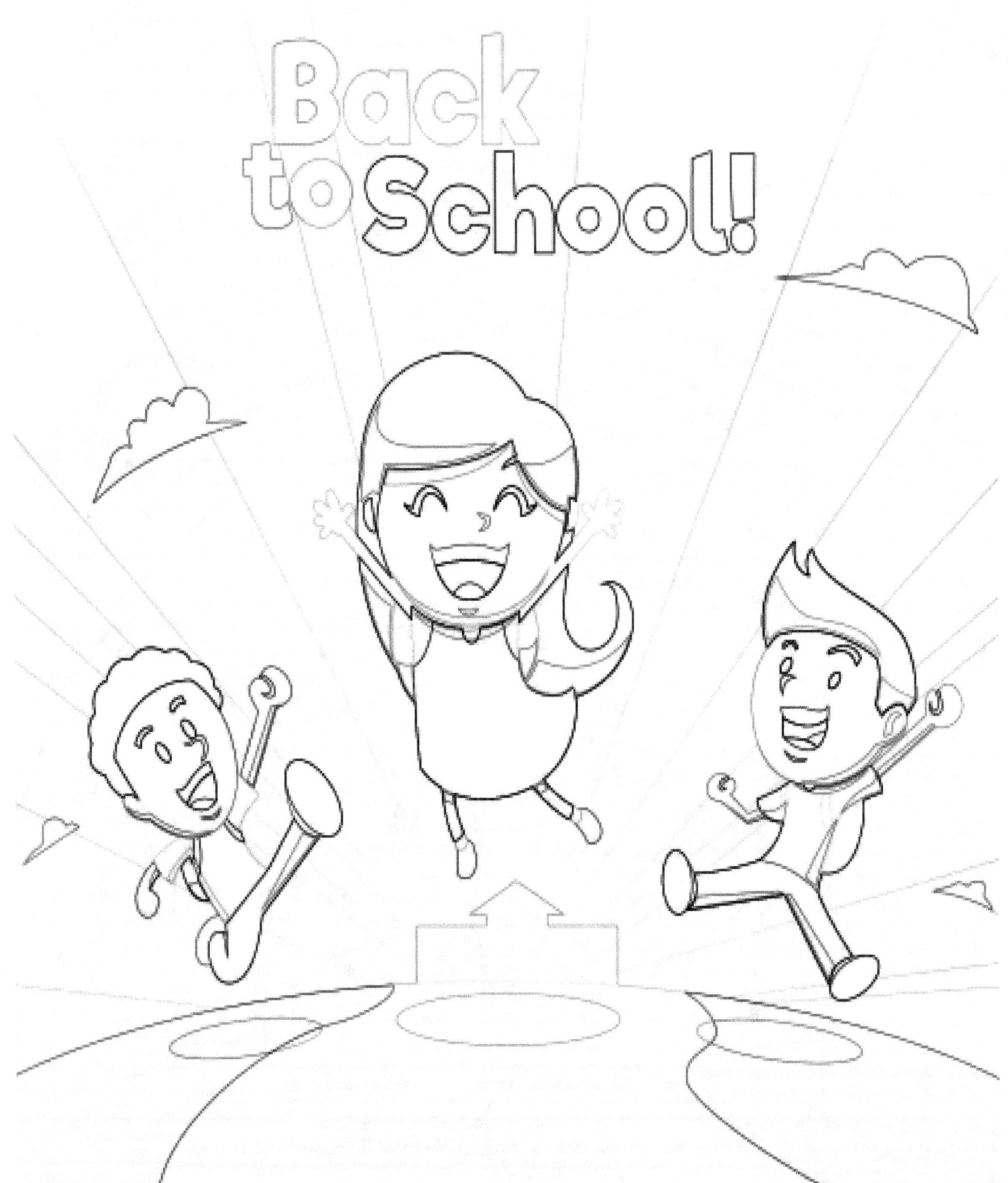

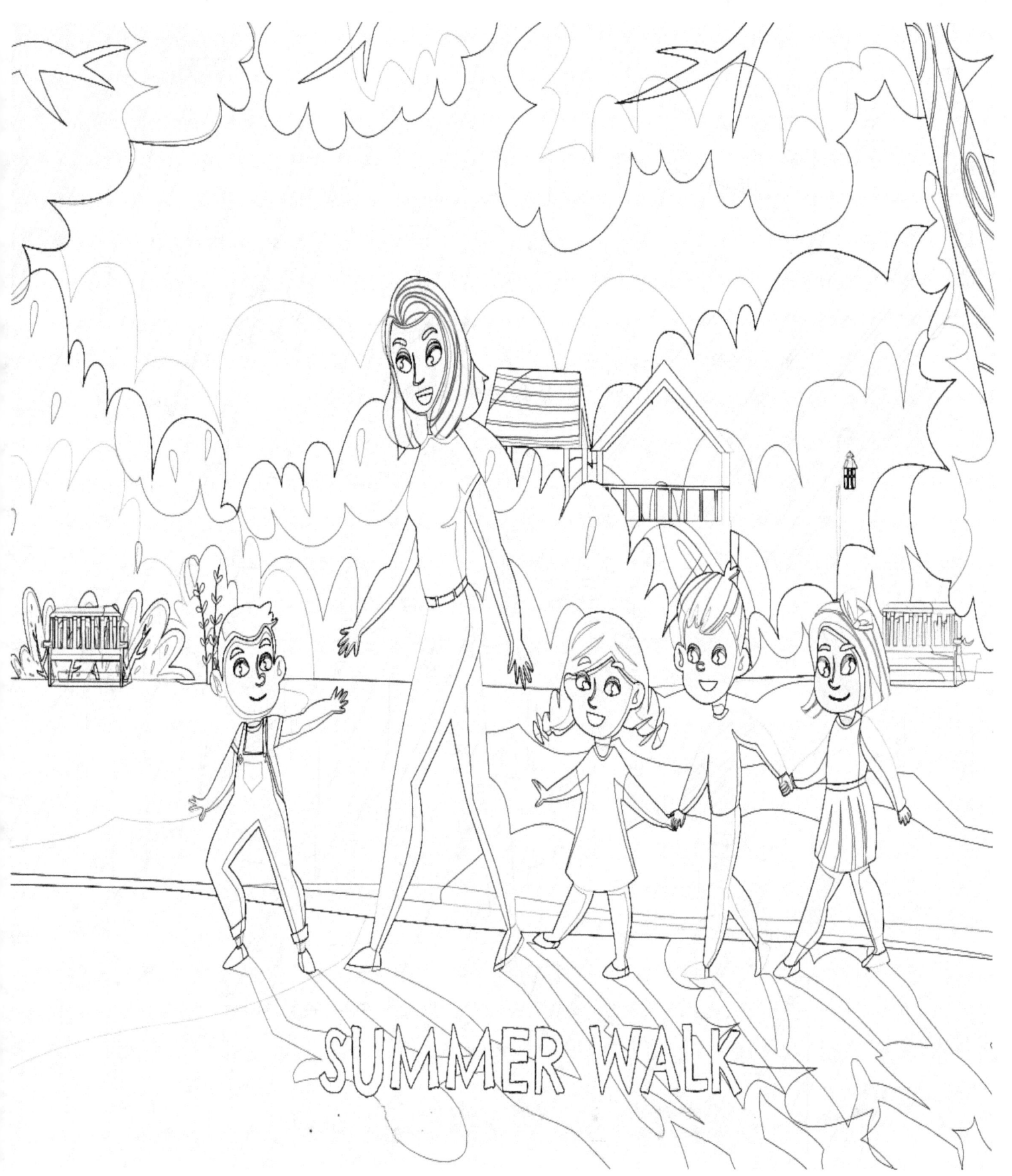

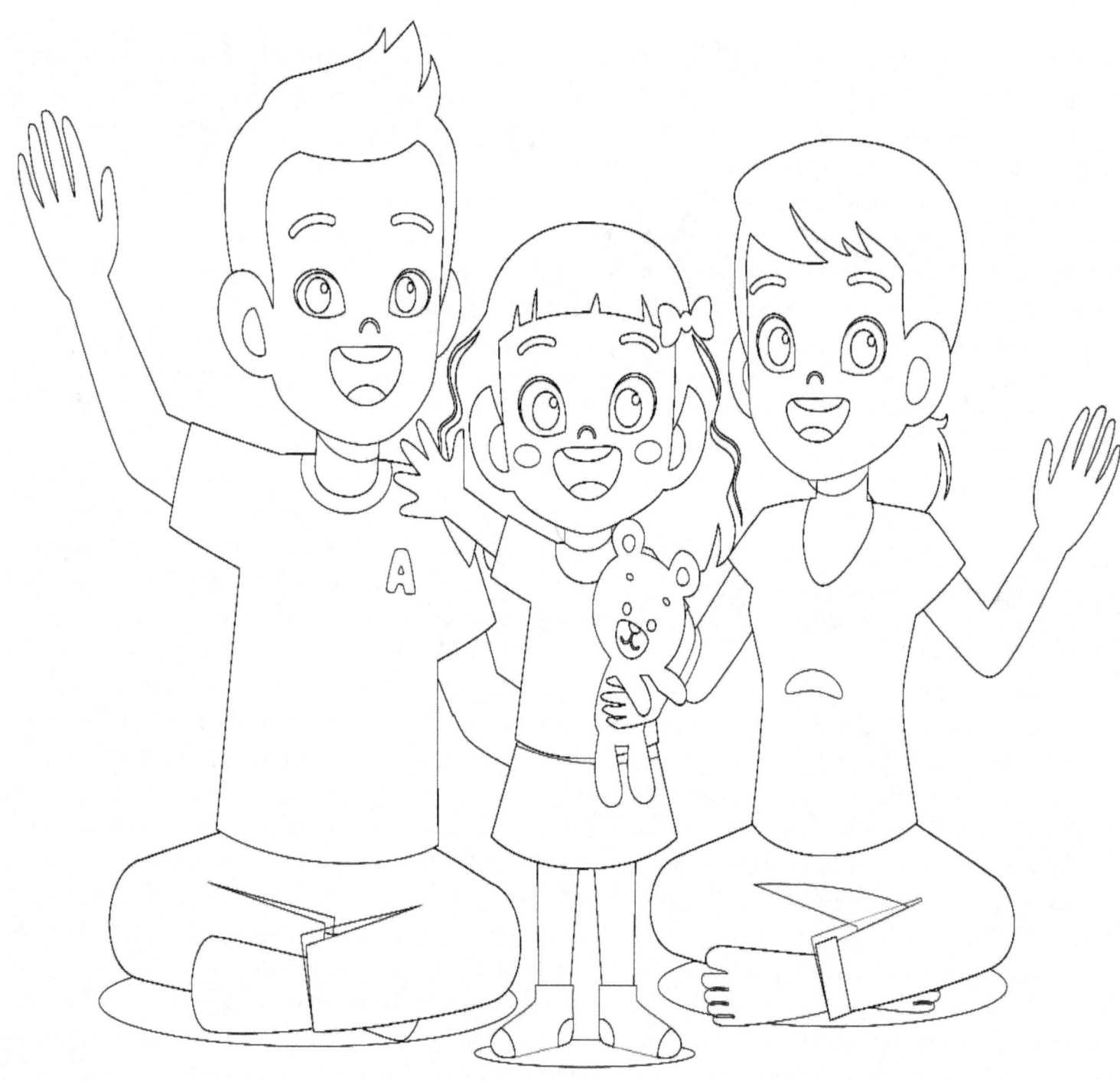

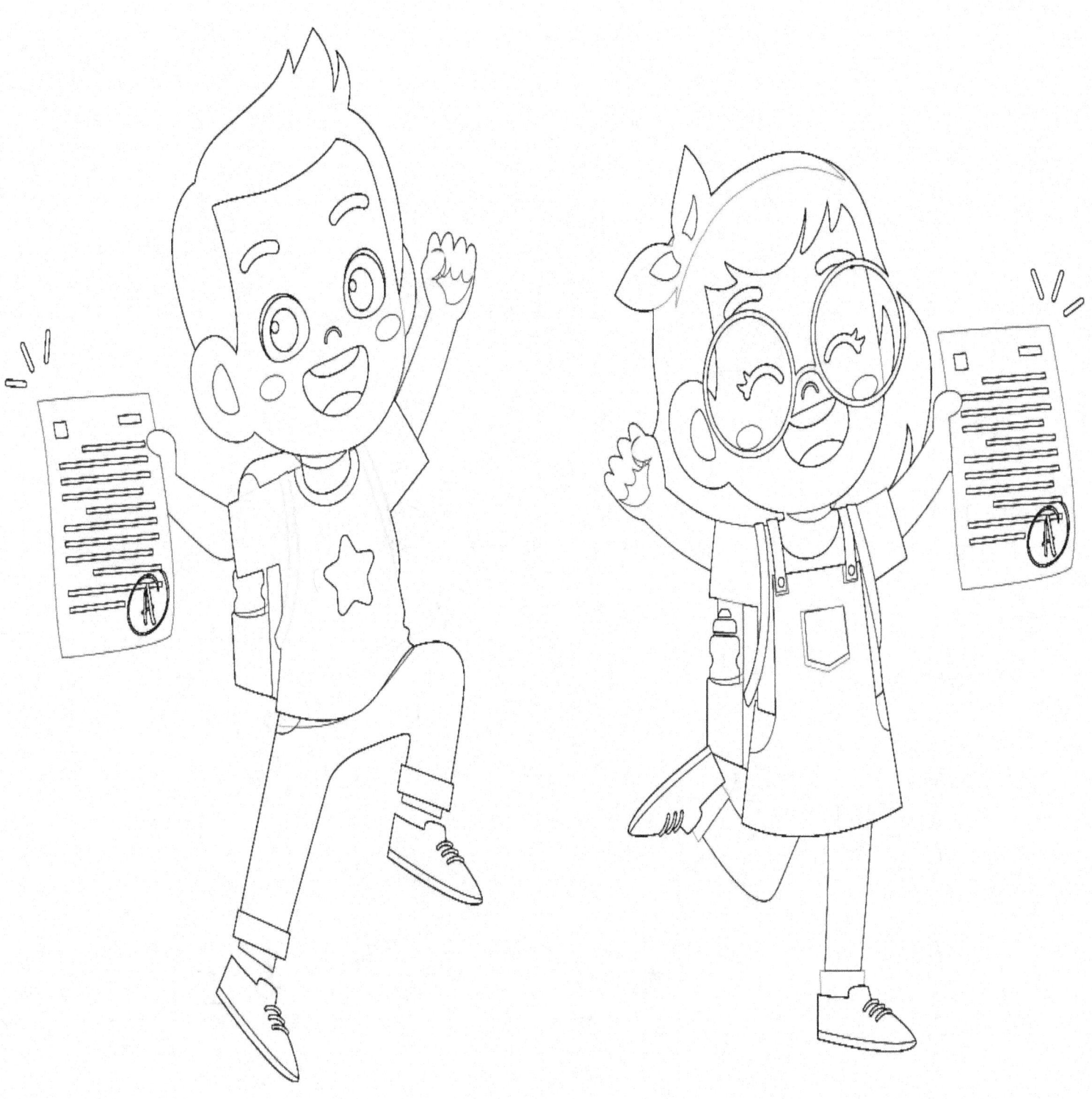

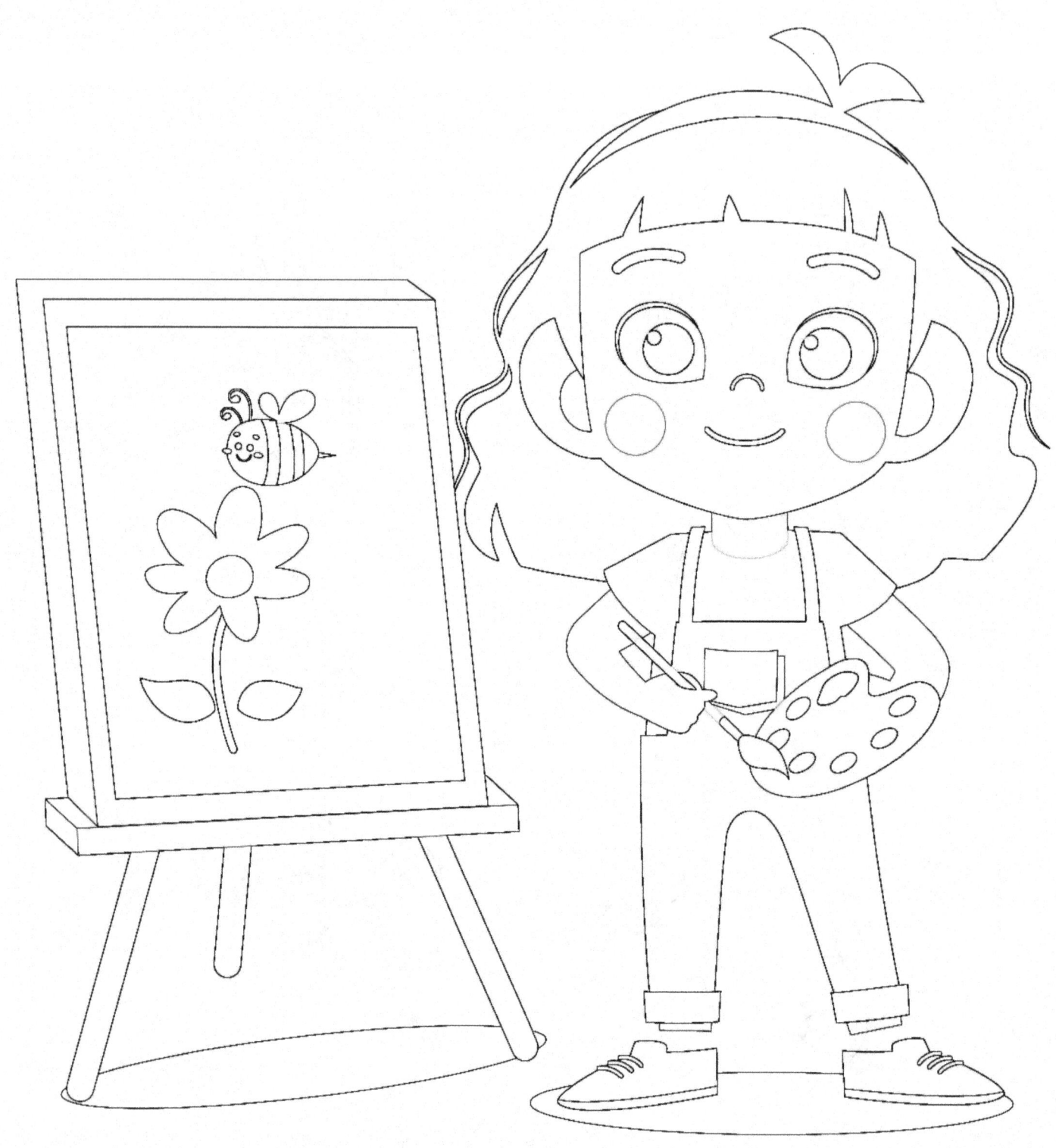

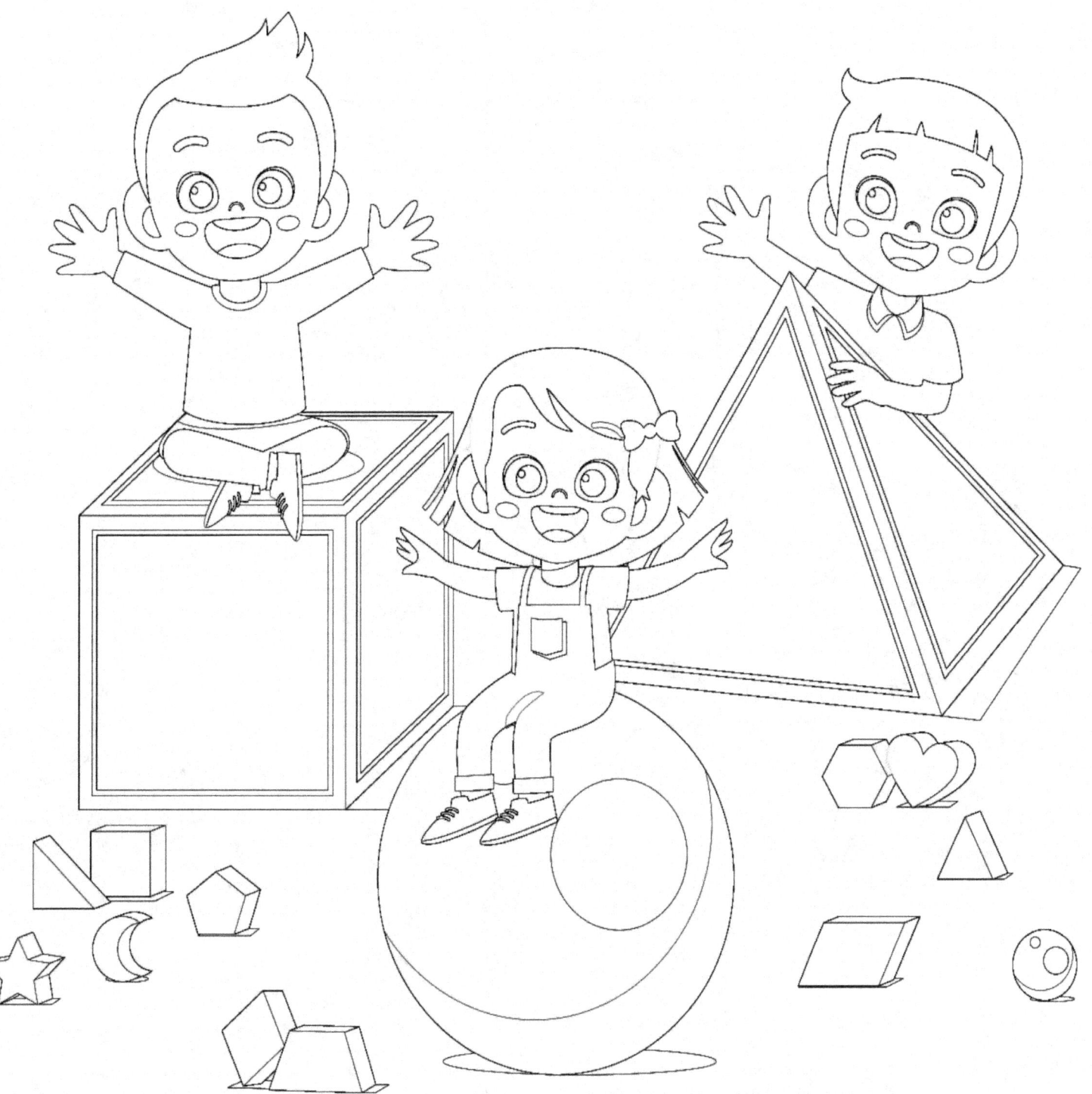

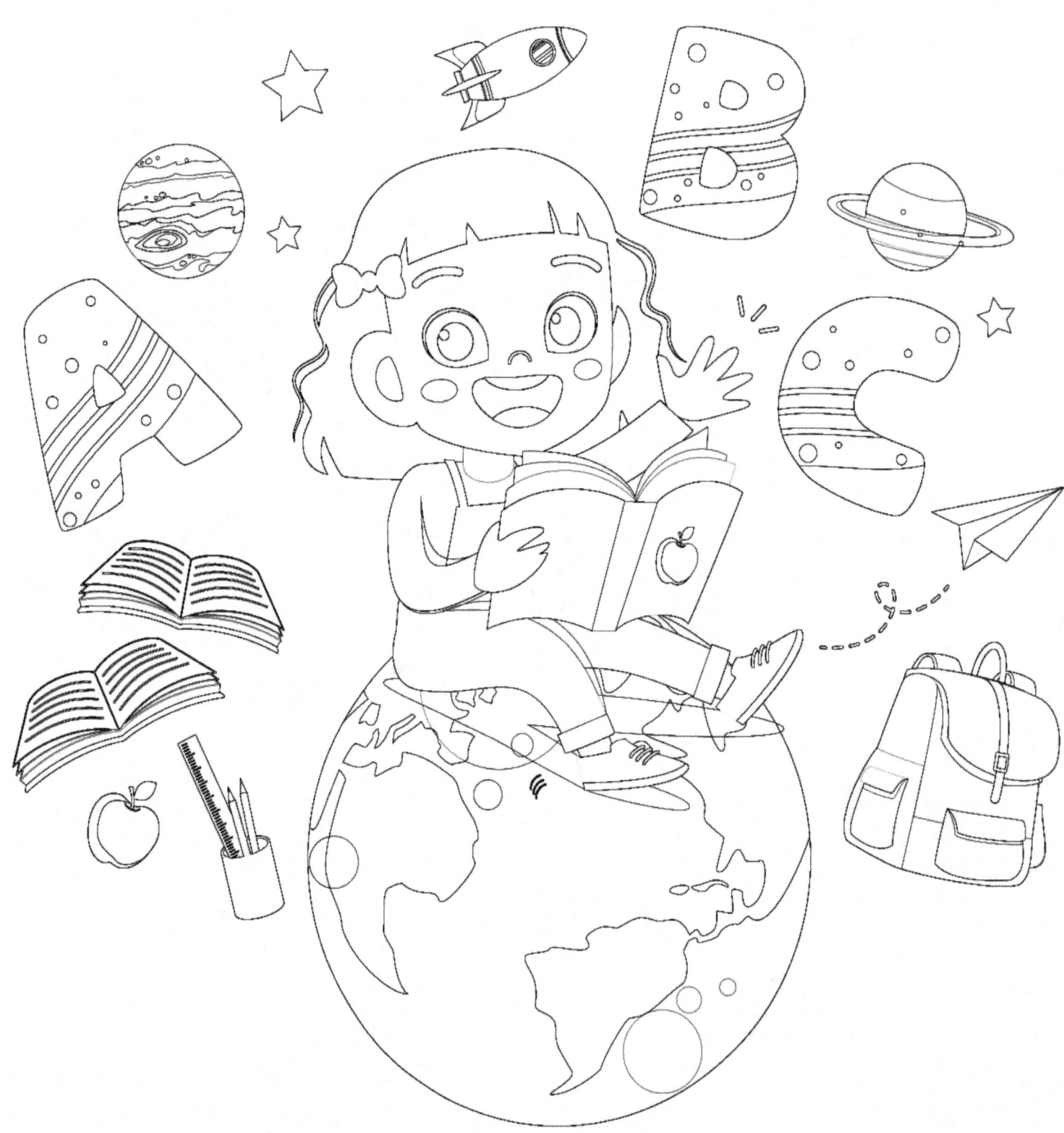

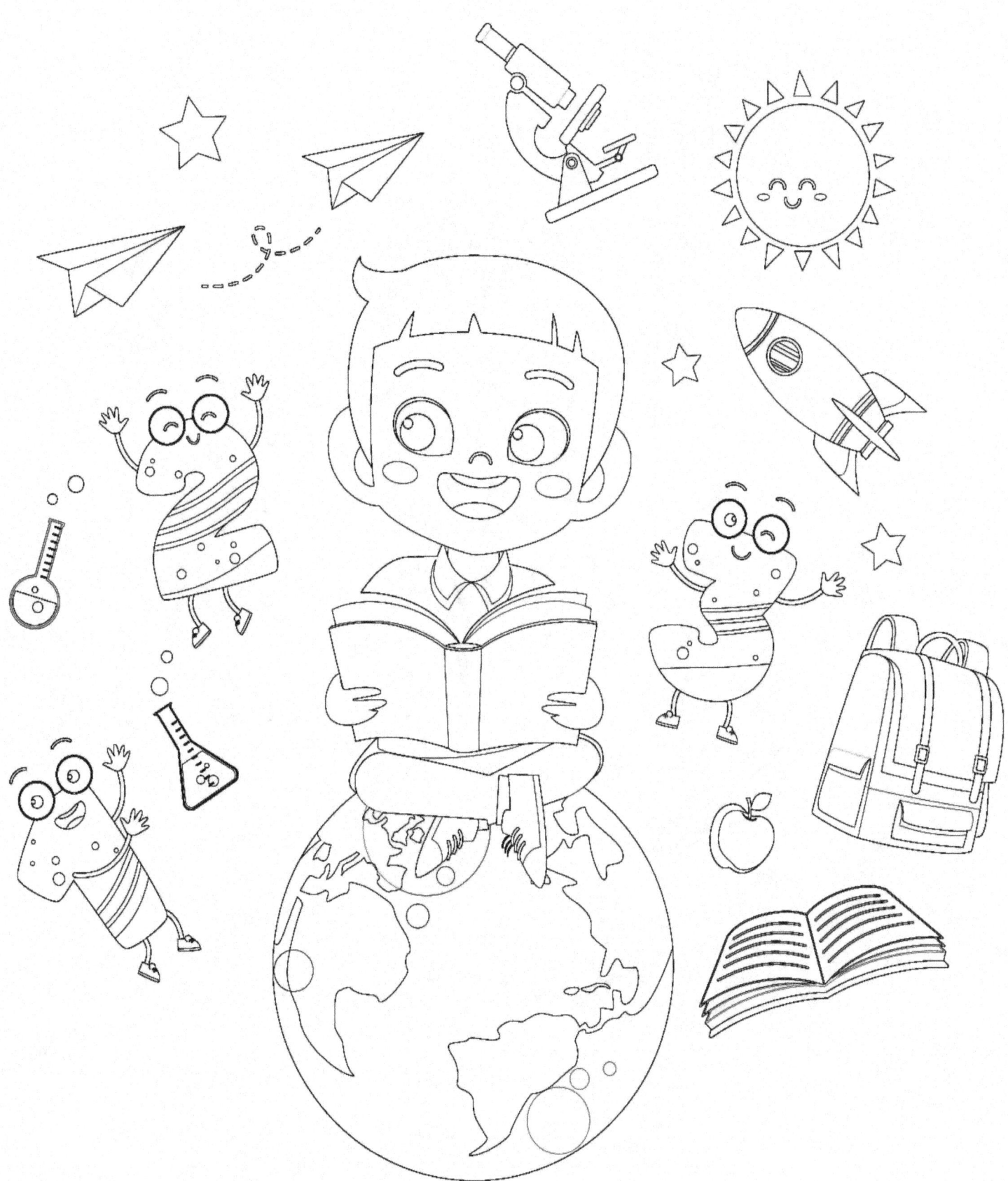

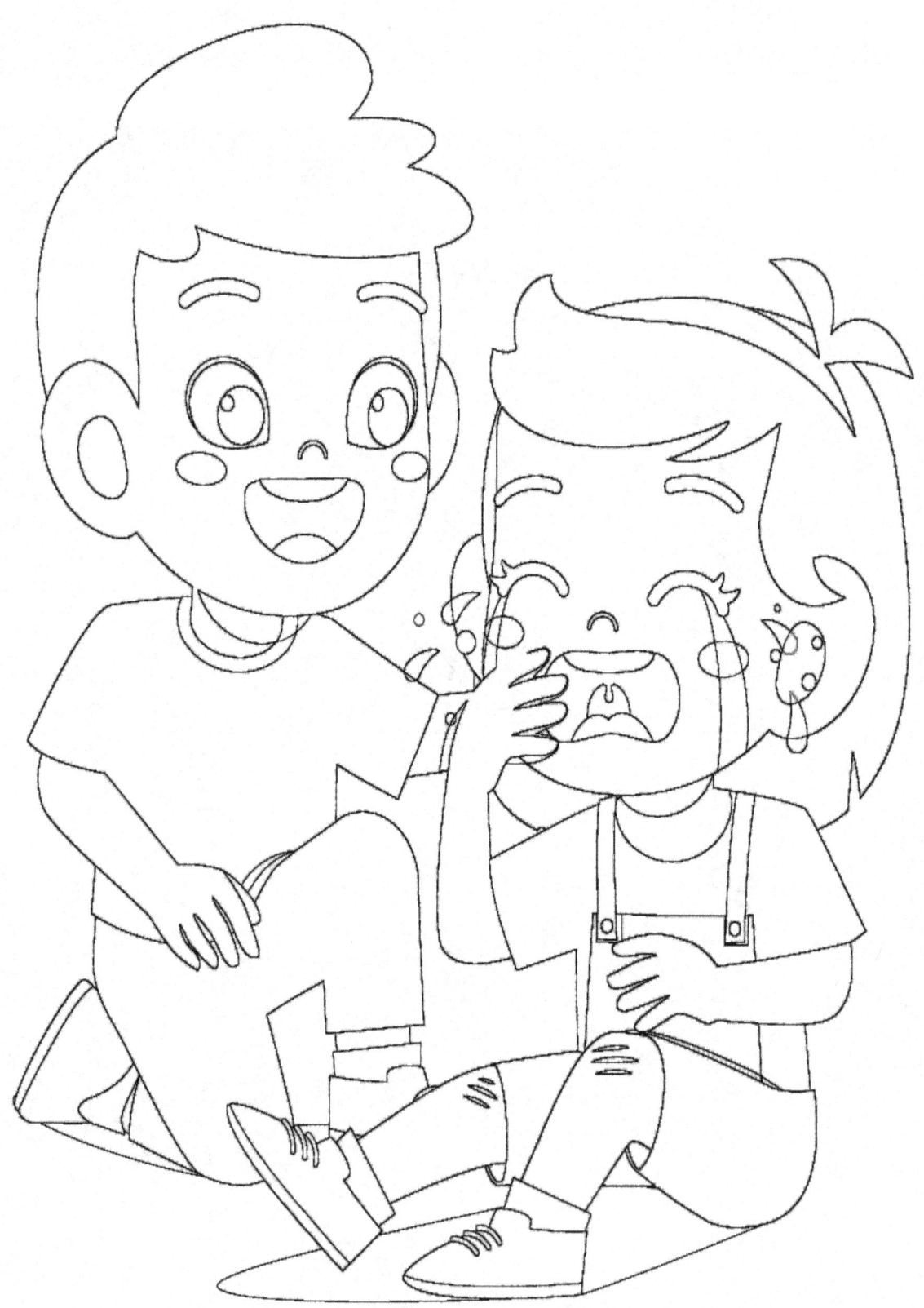

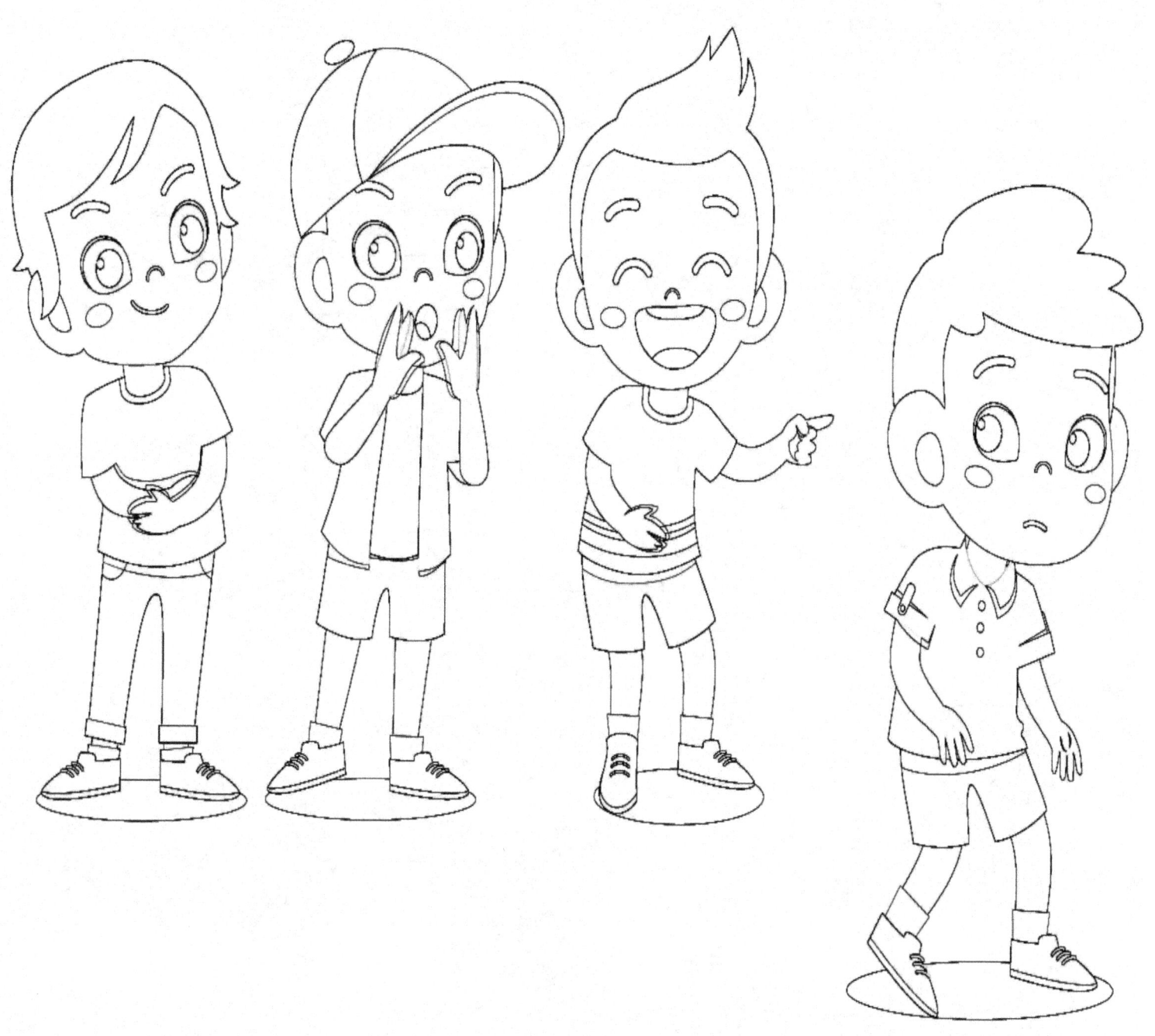

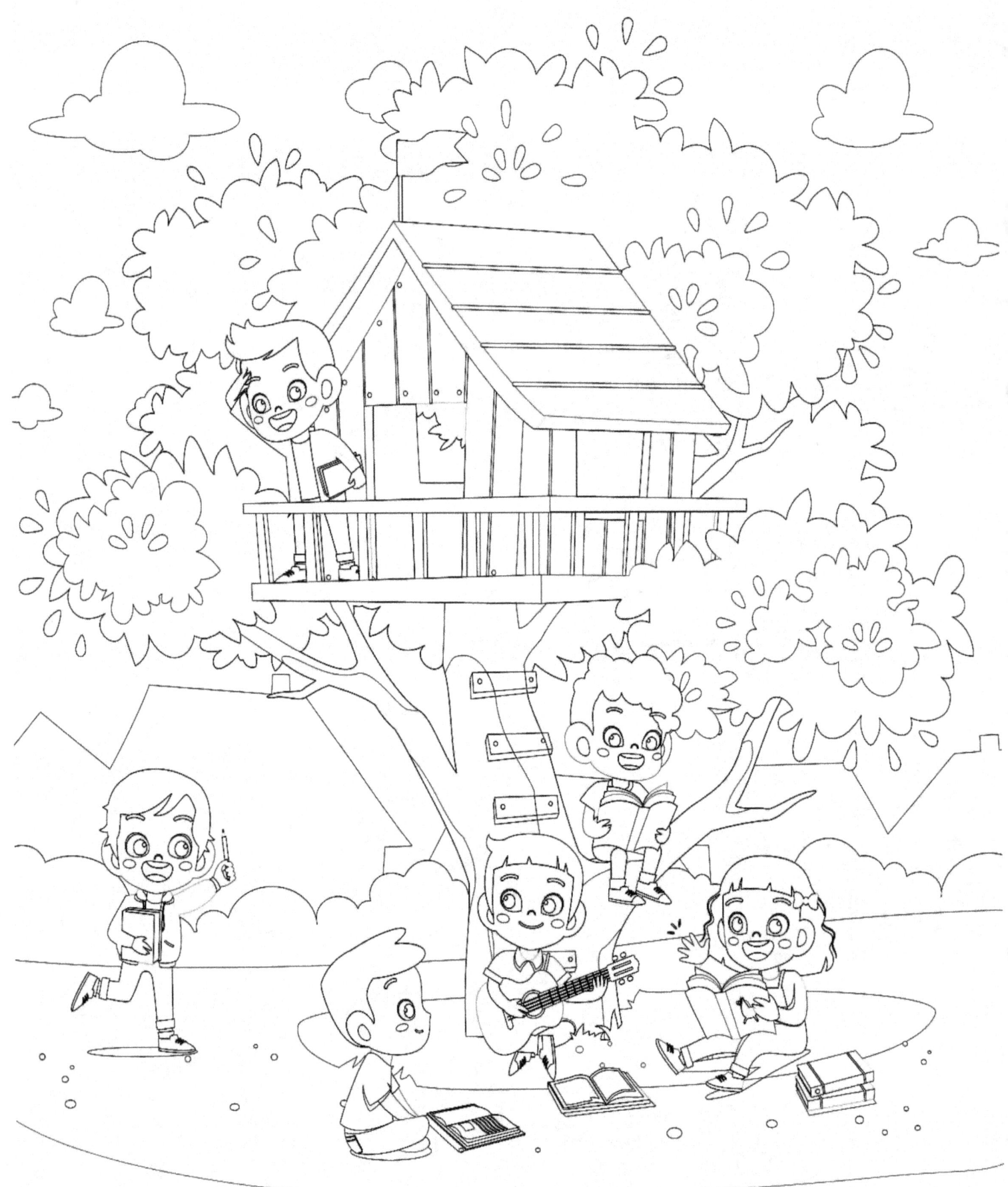

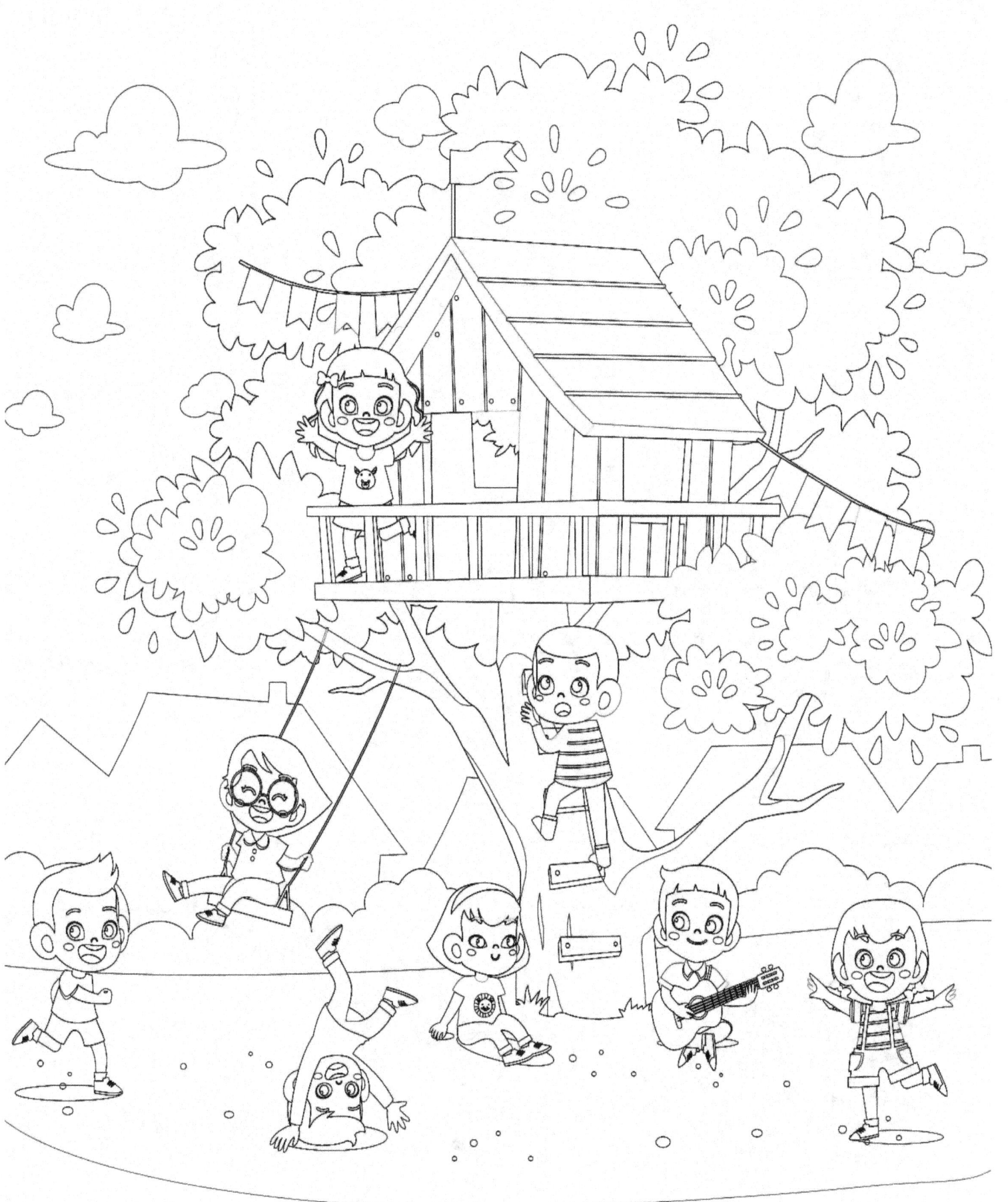

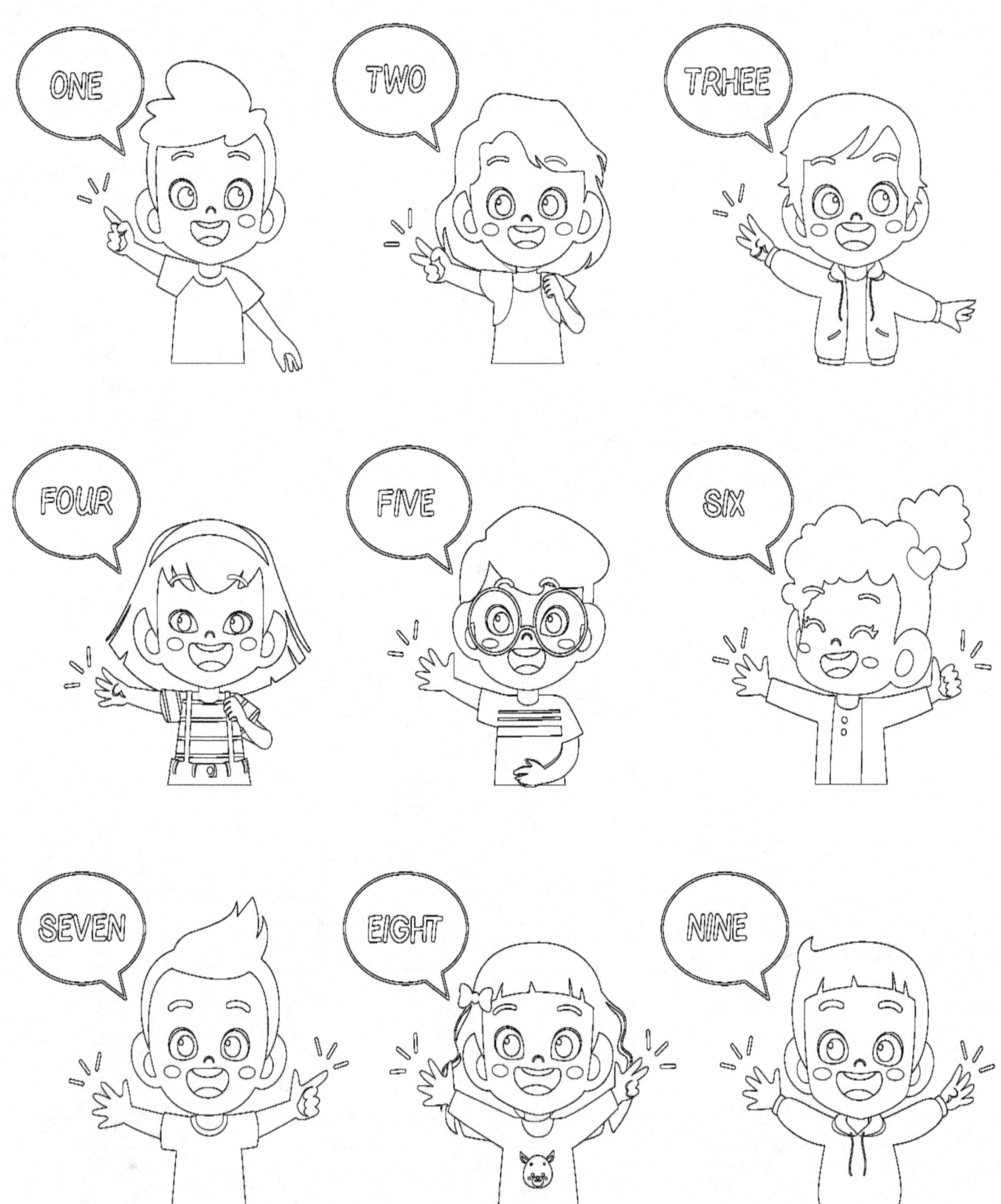

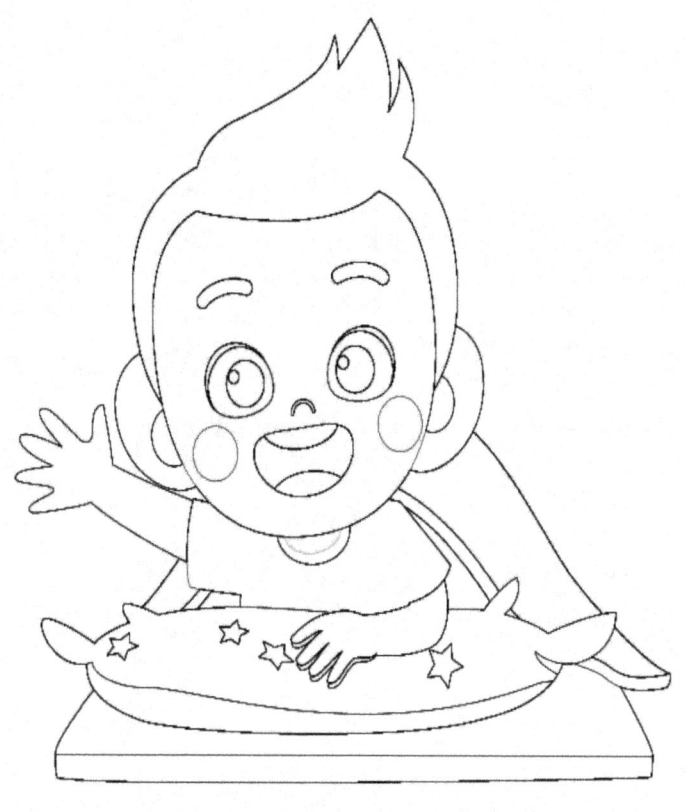
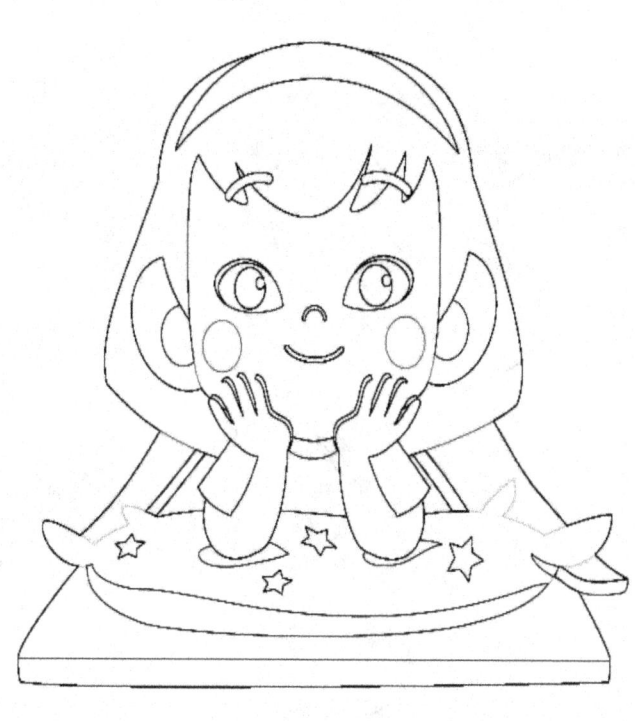
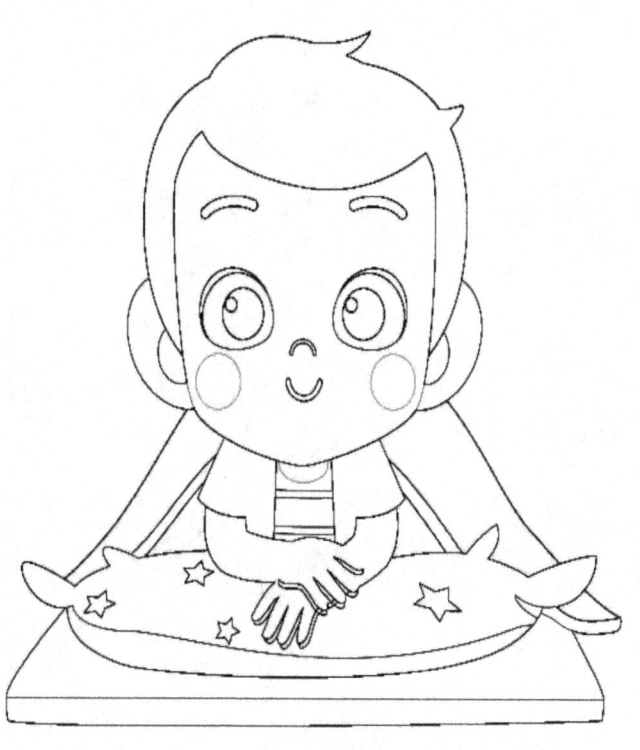
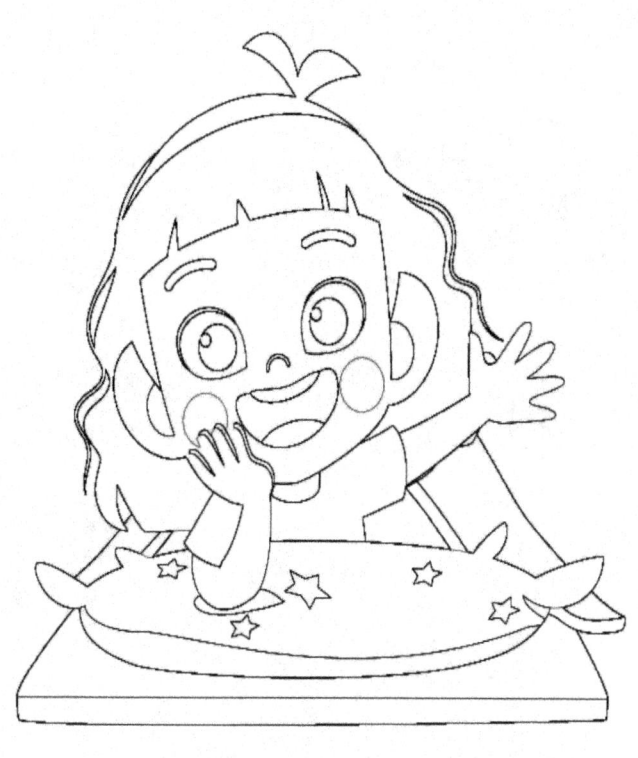

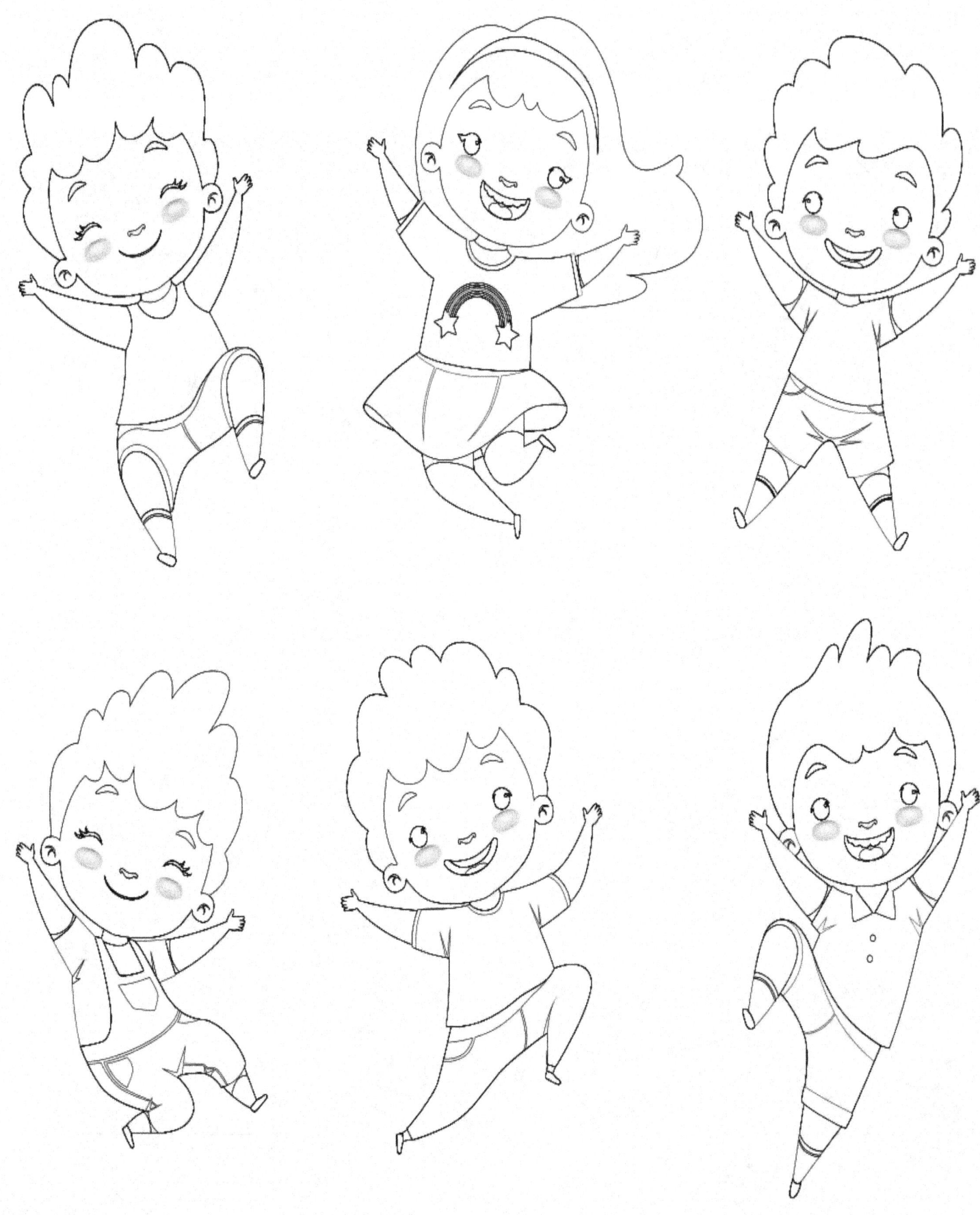

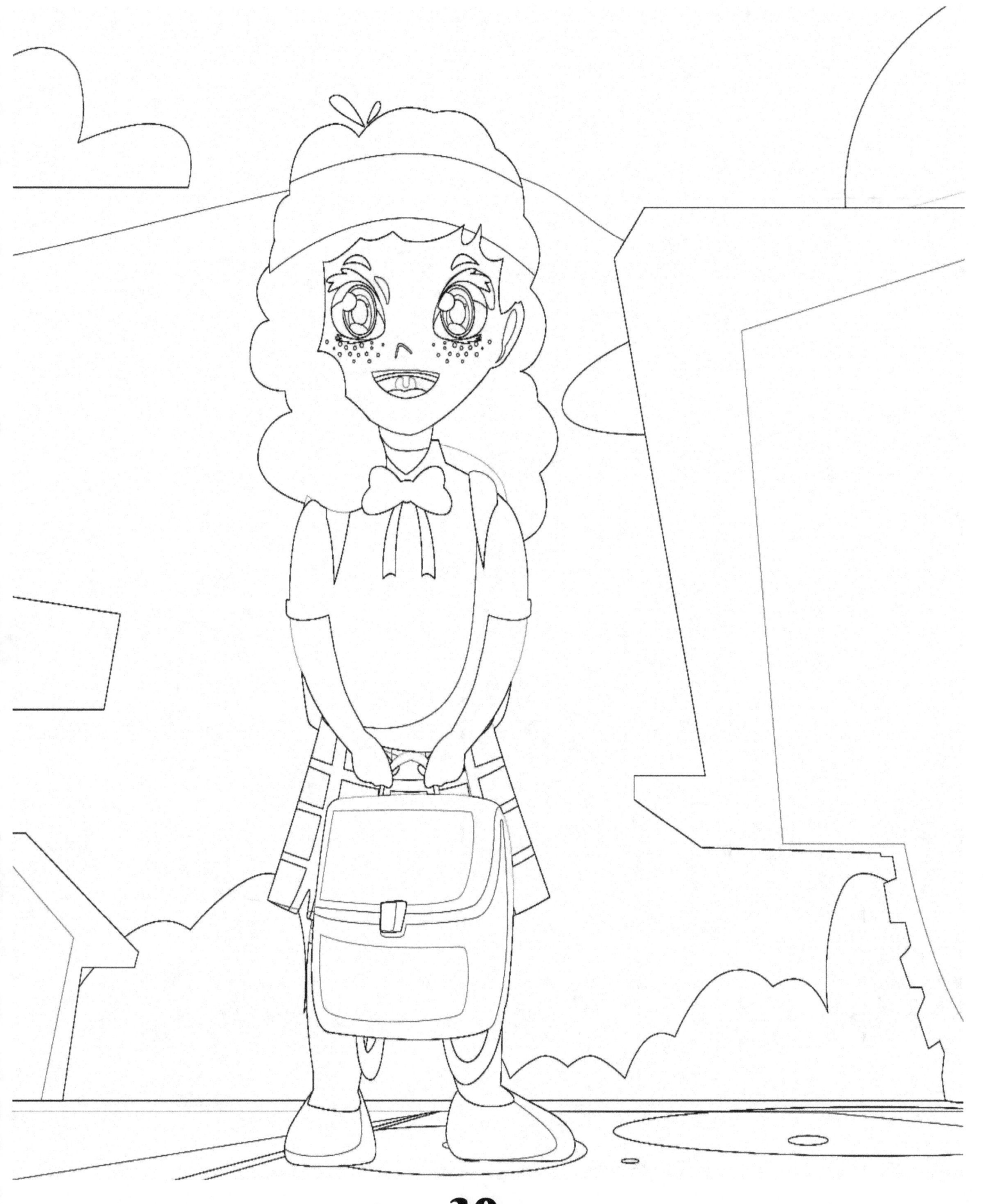

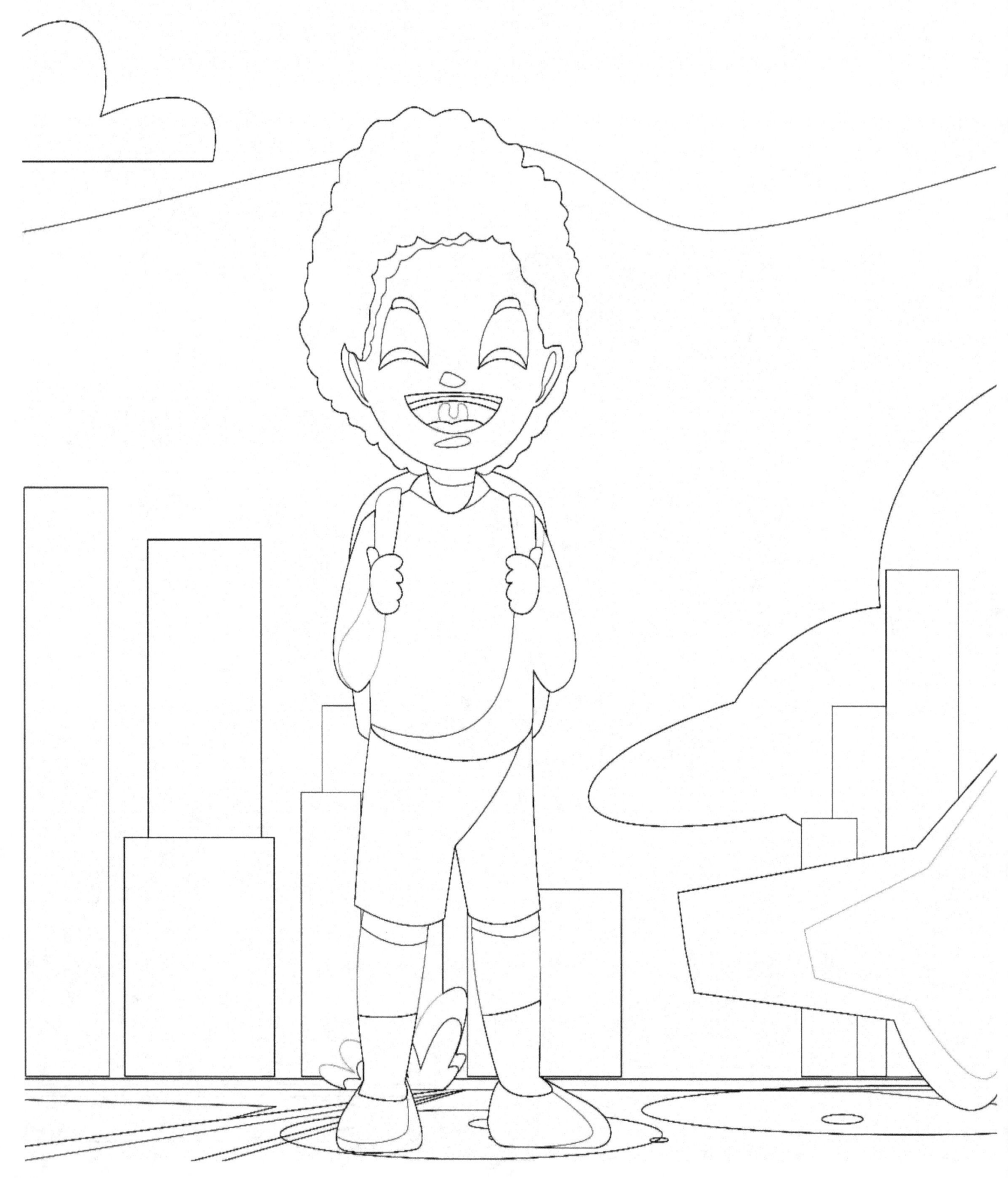

.31.

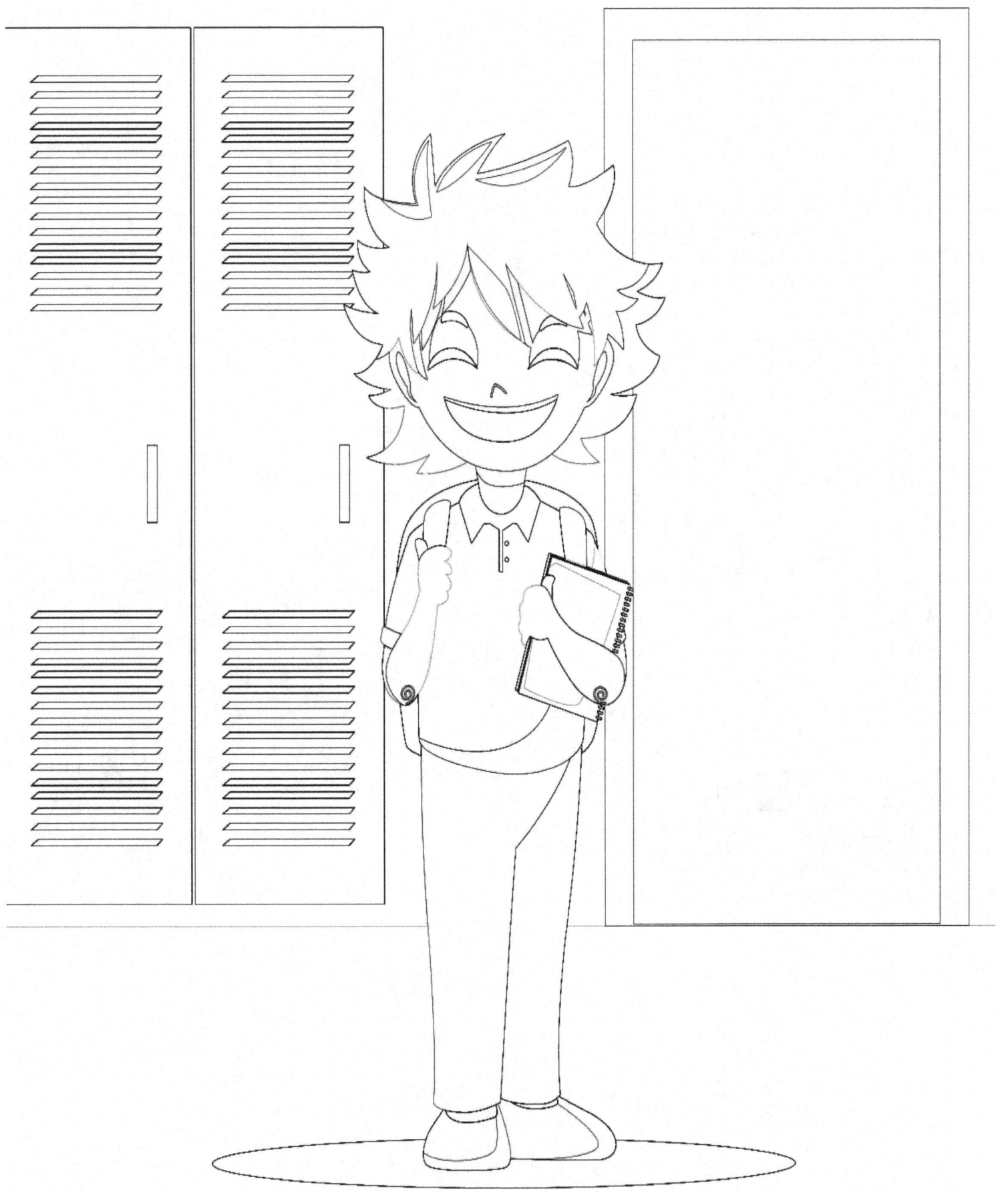

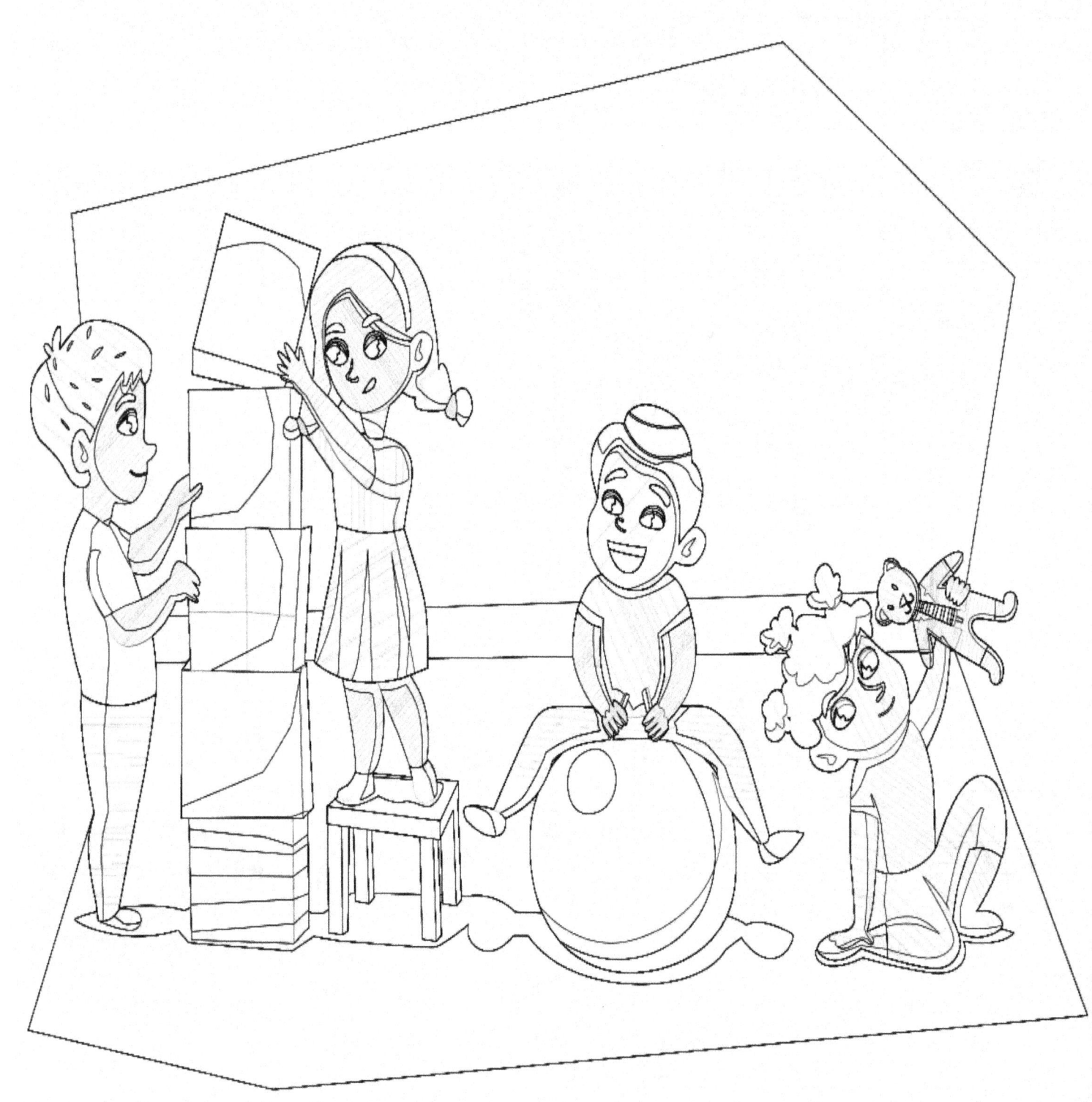

GAME ROOM

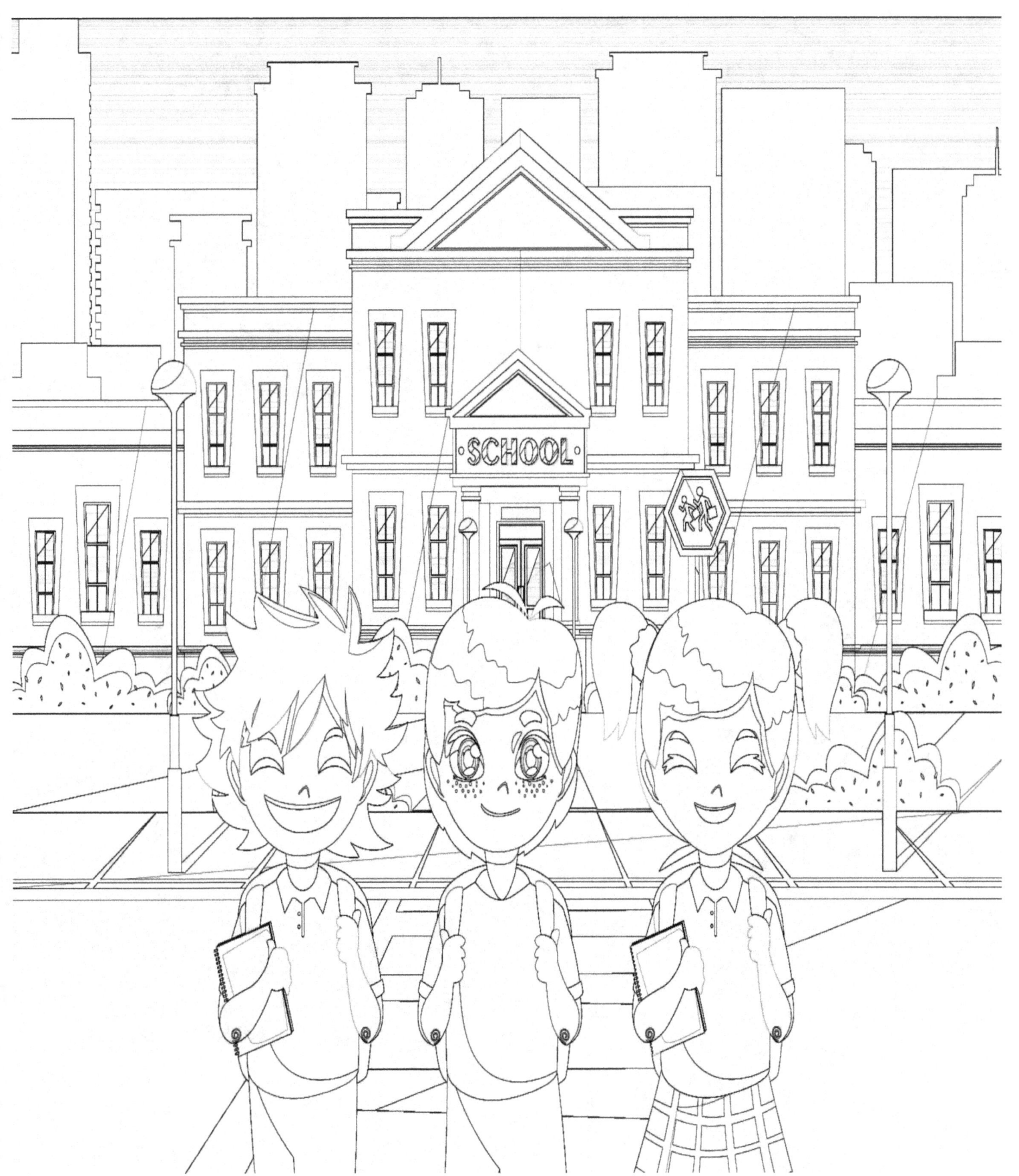

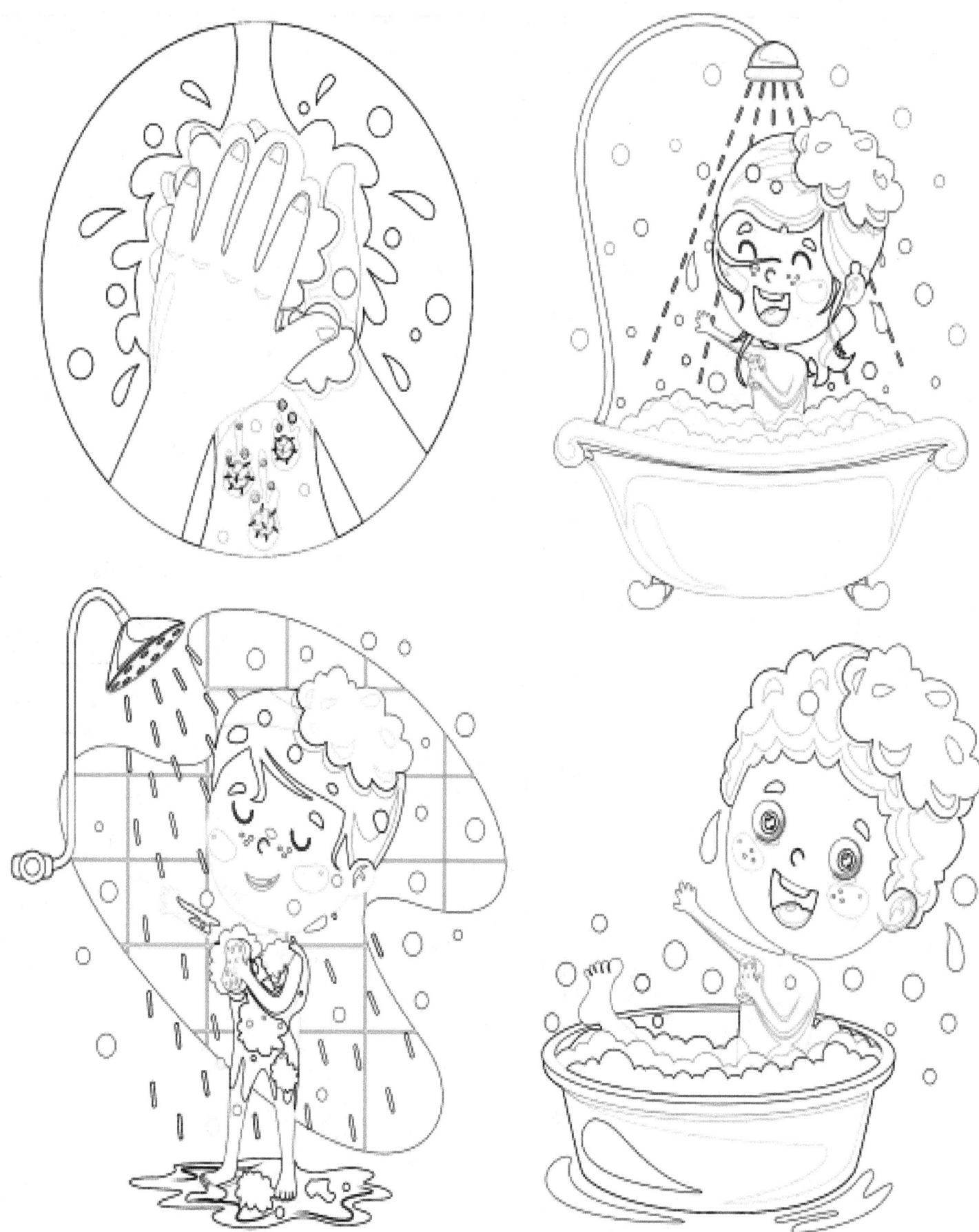

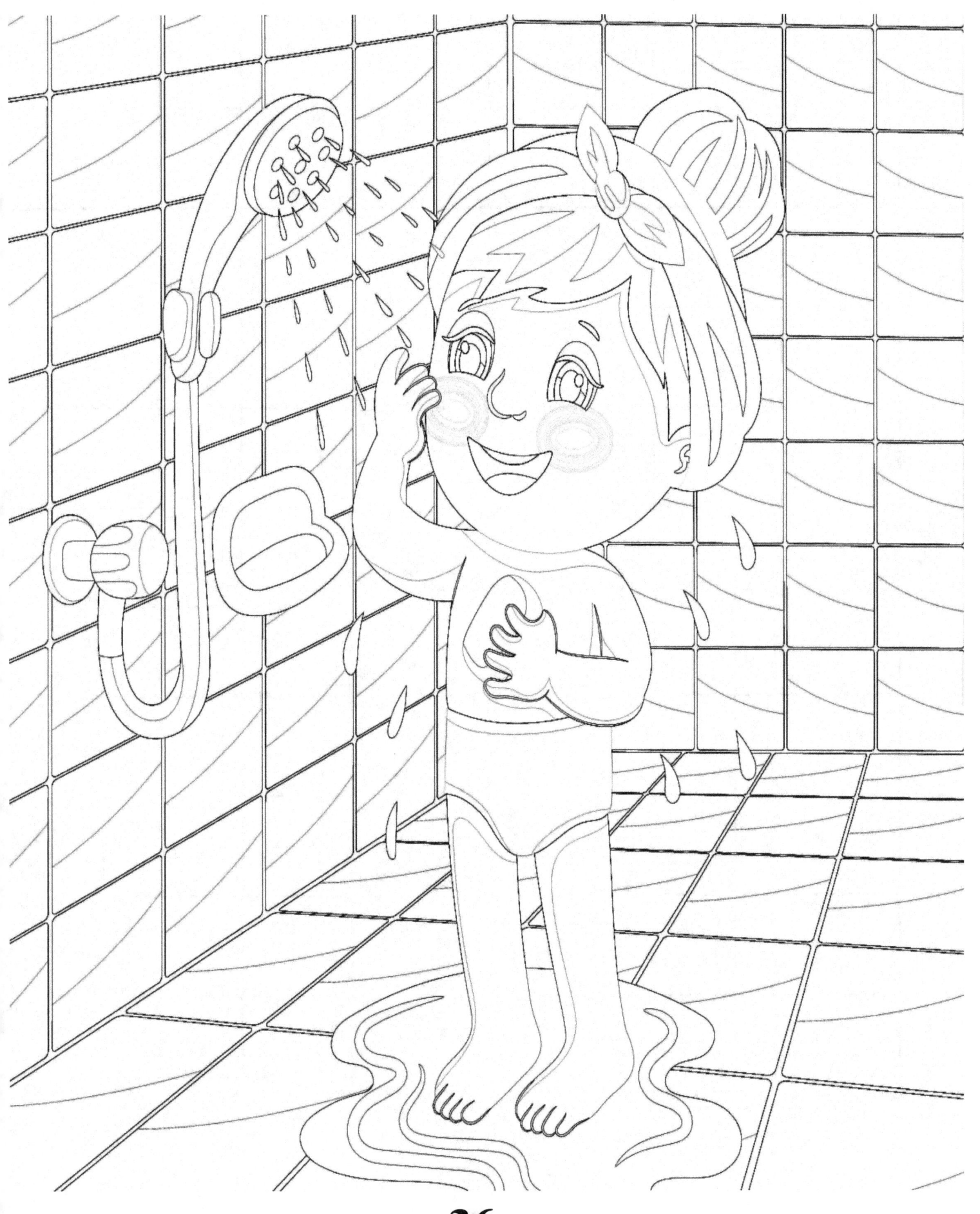

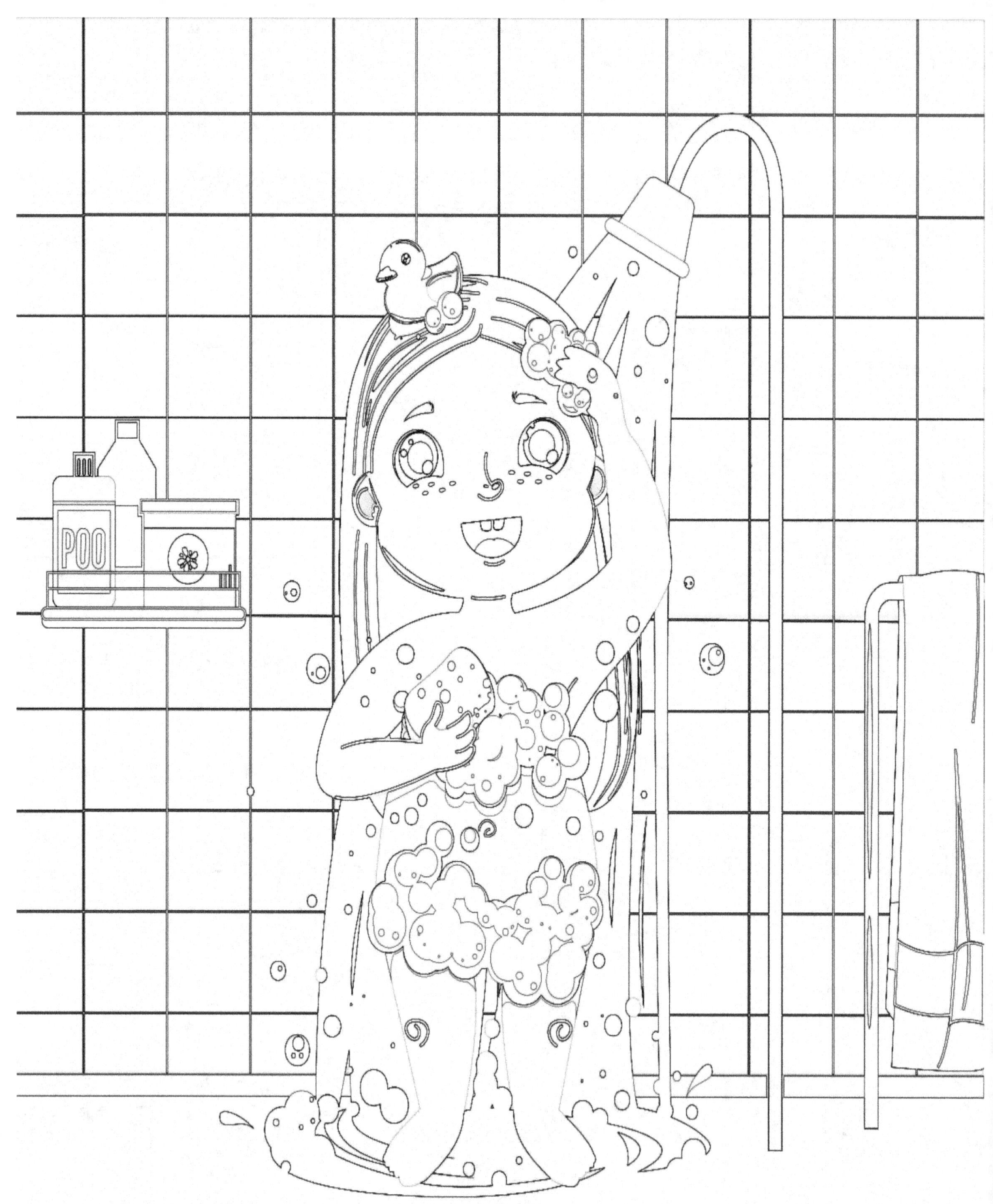

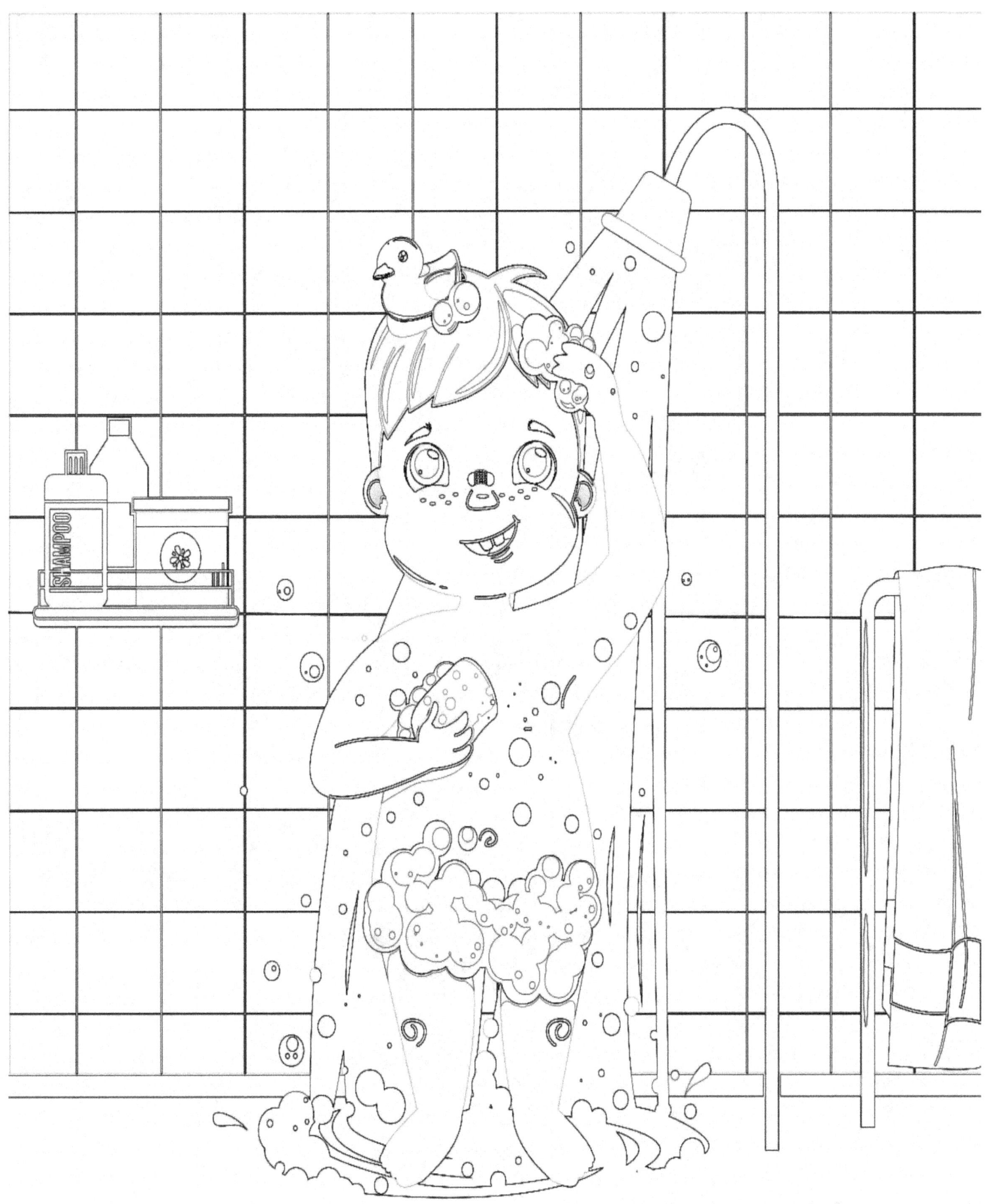

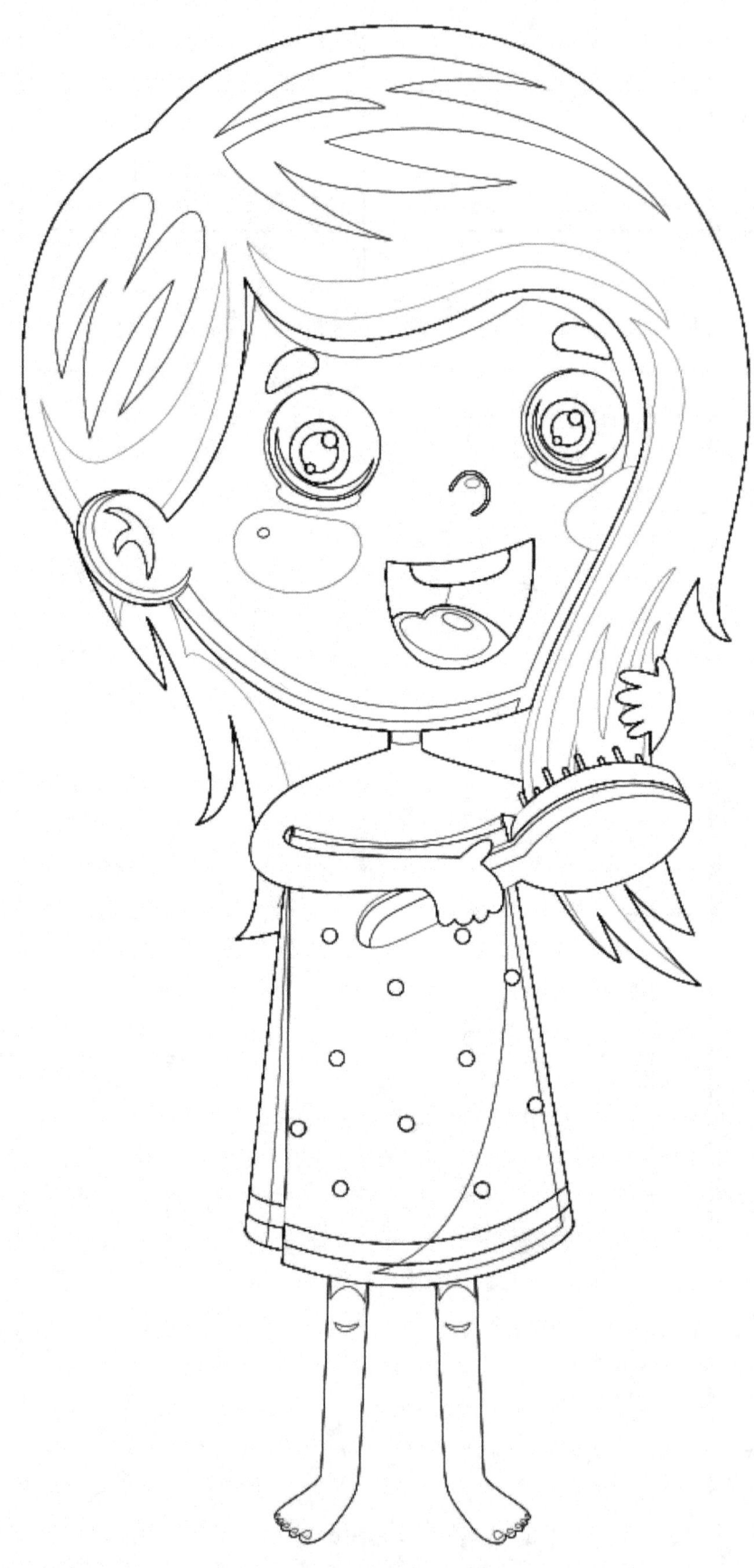

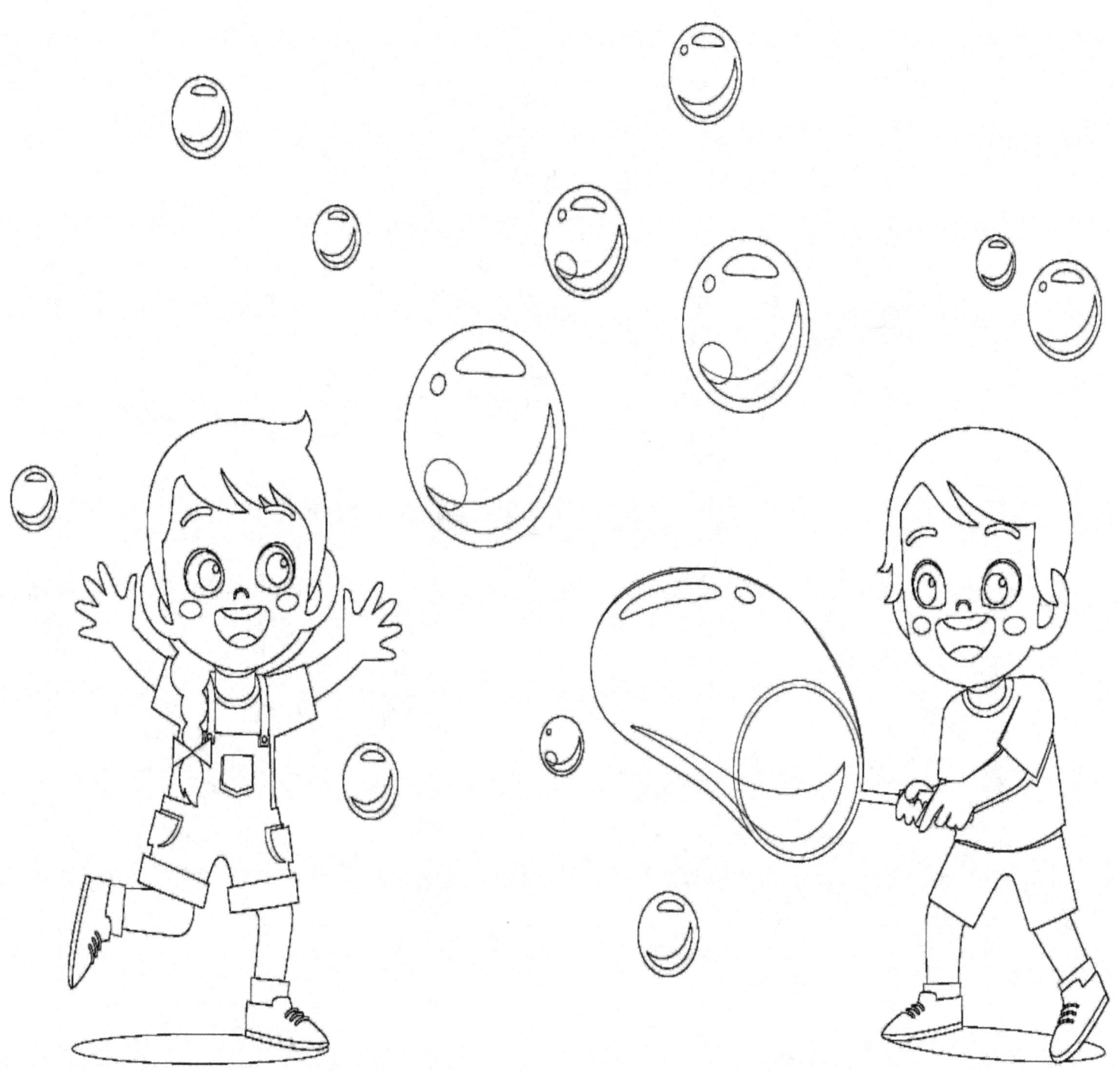

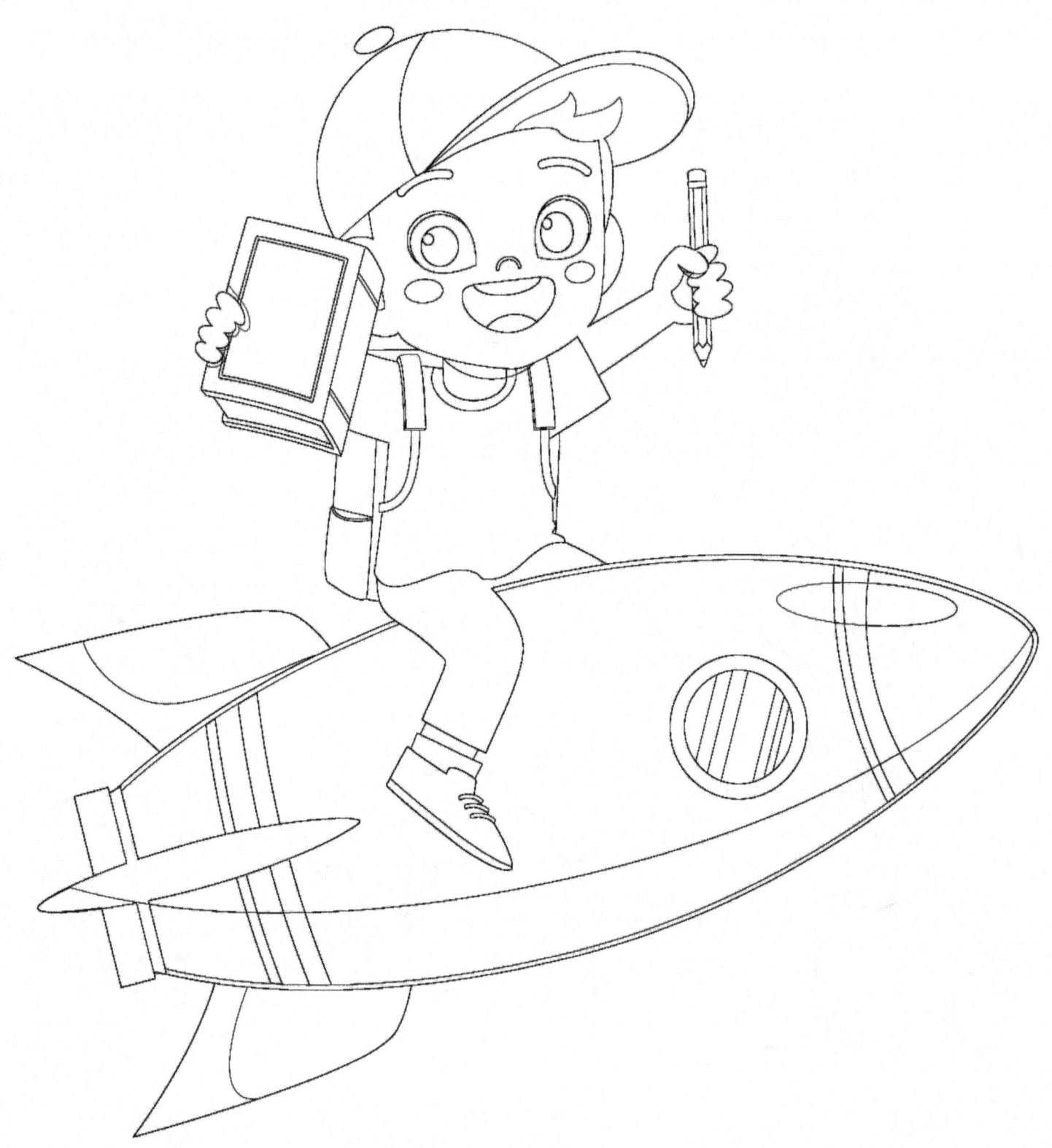

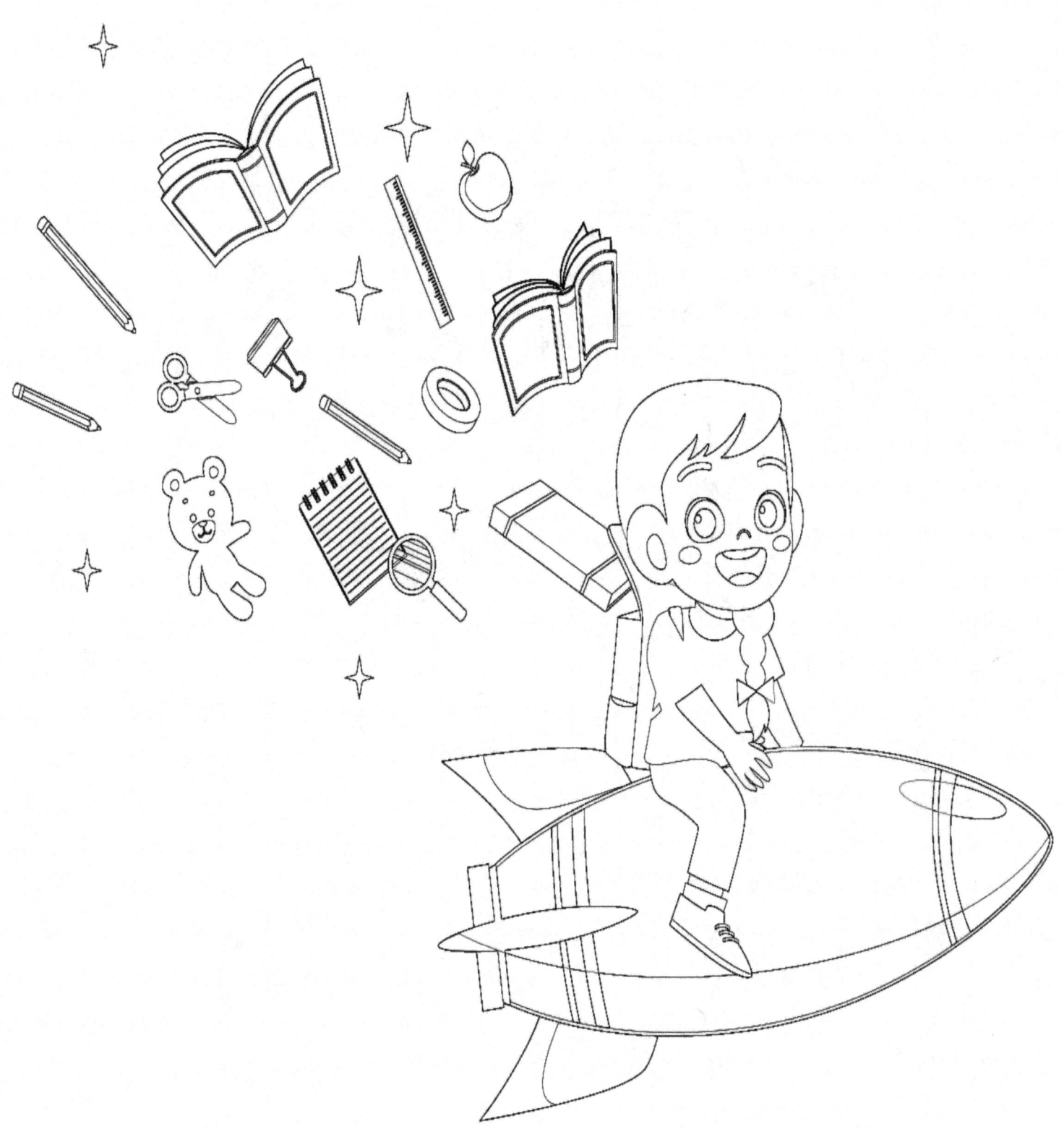

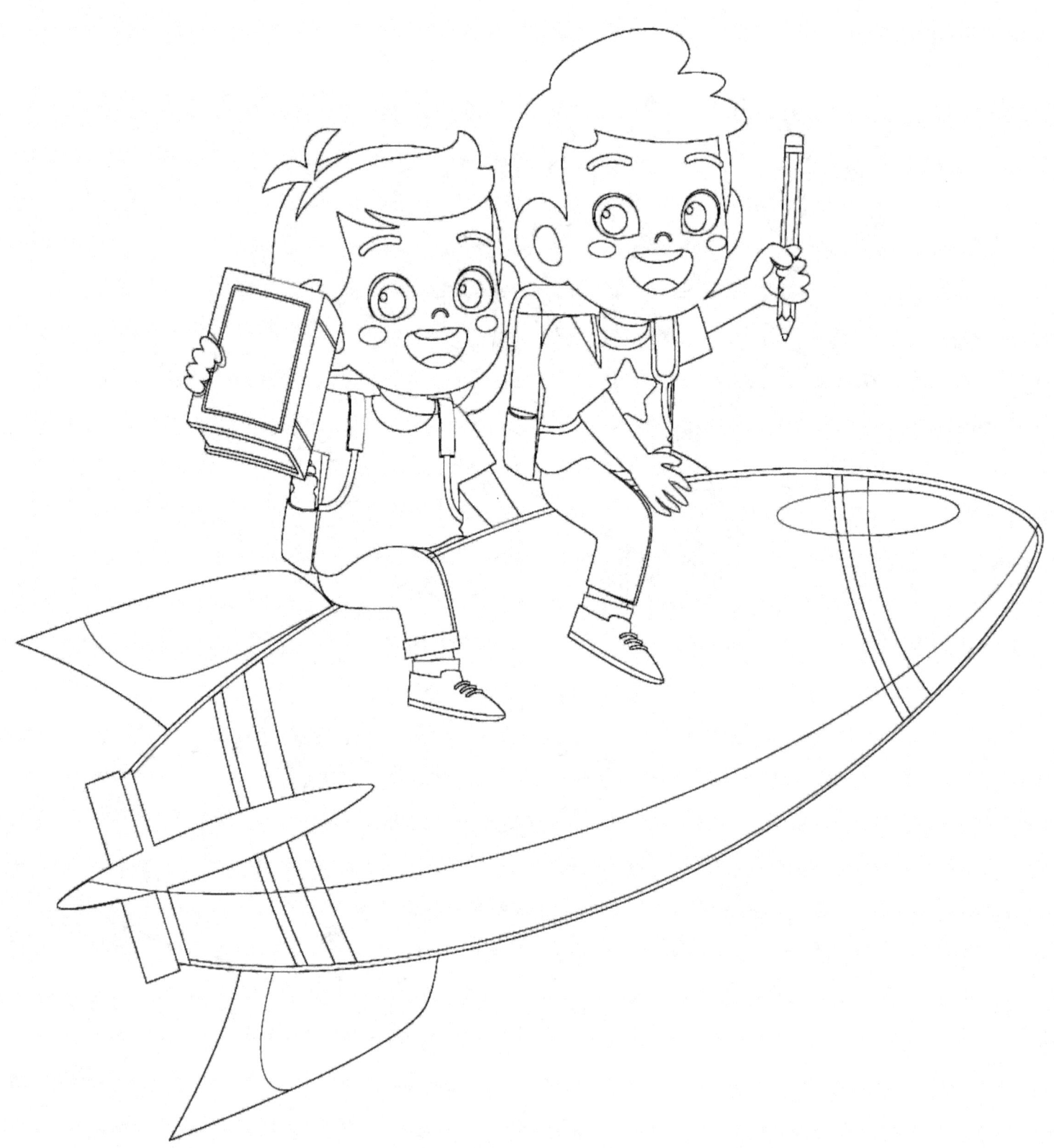

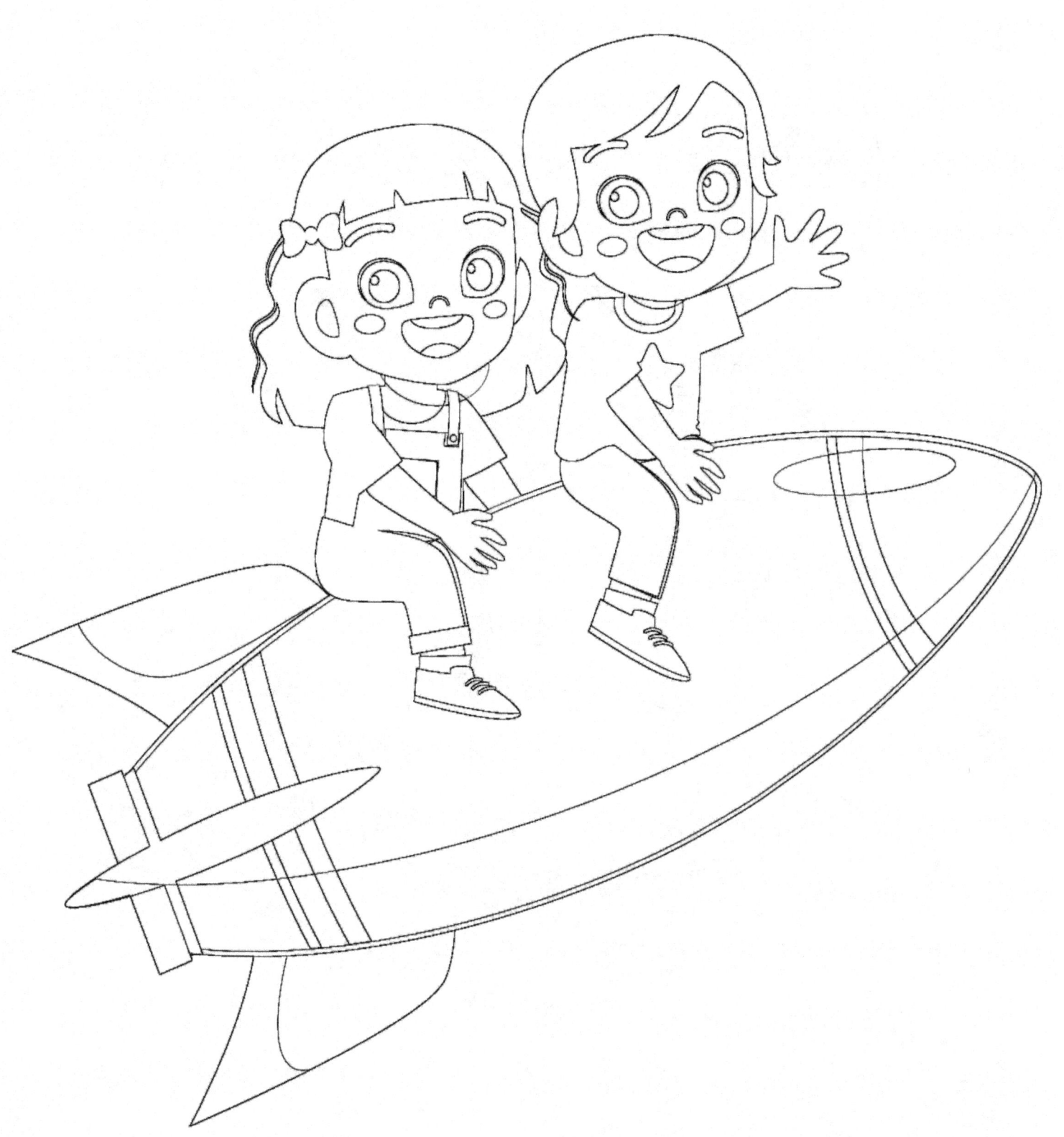

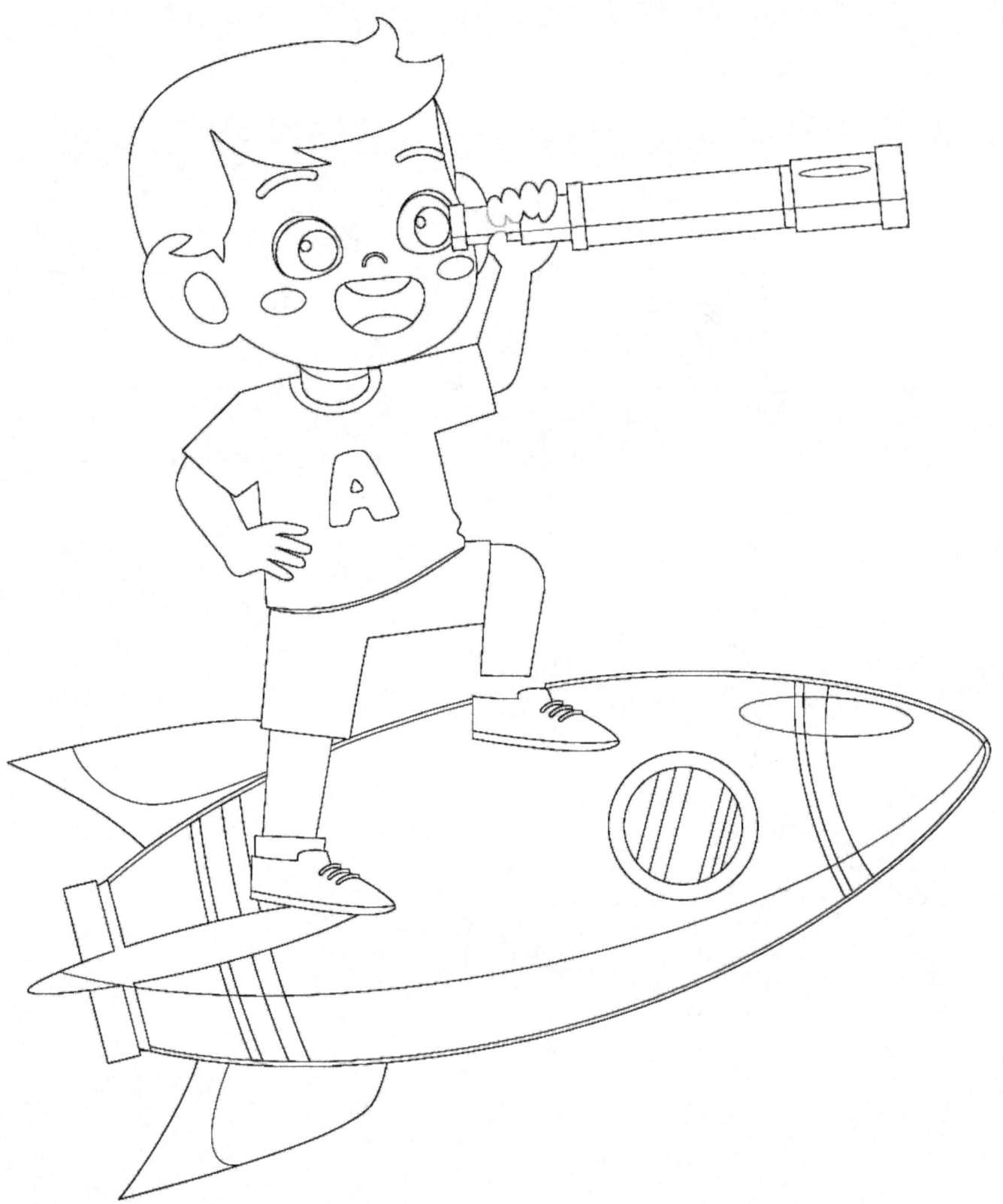

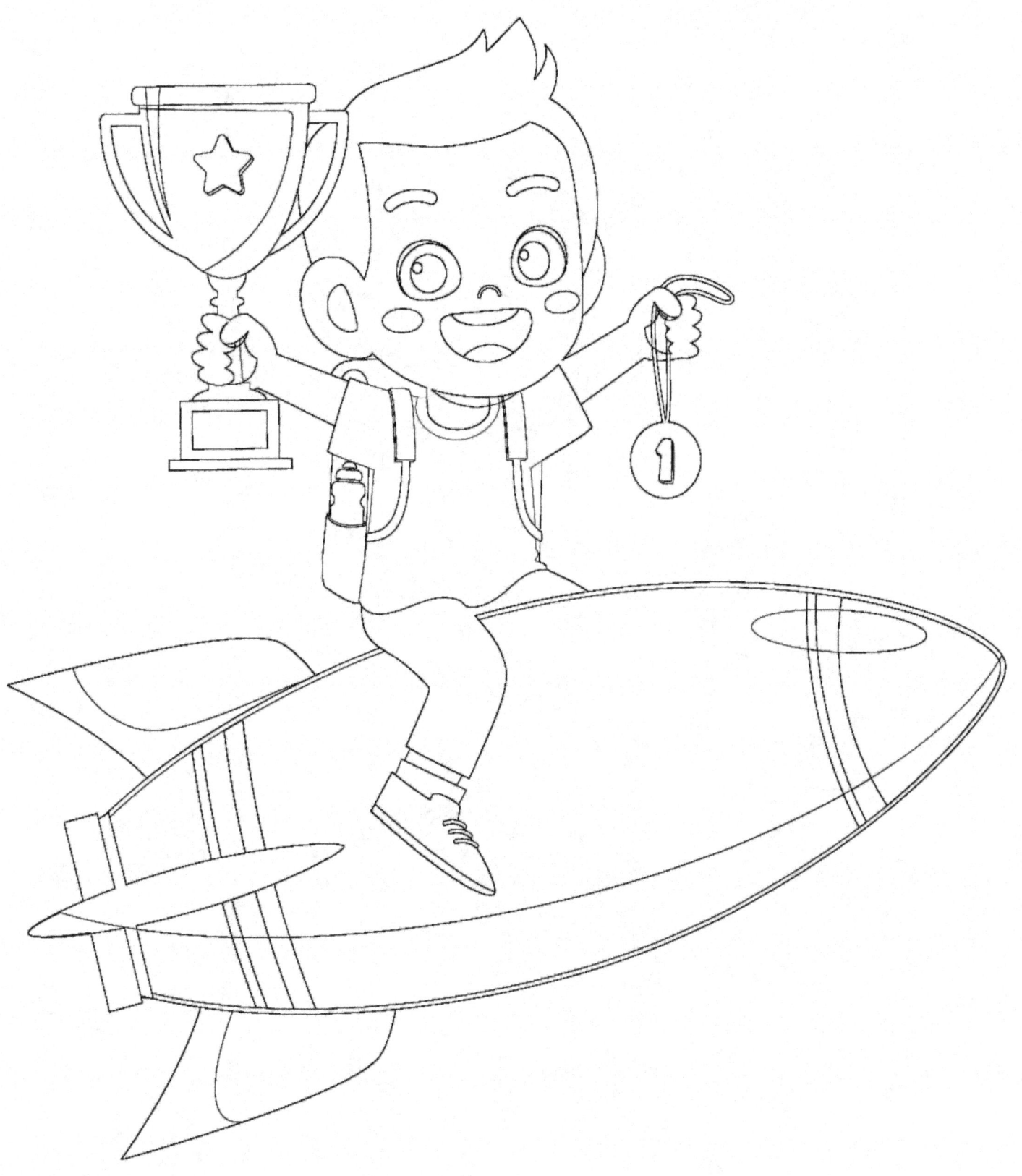

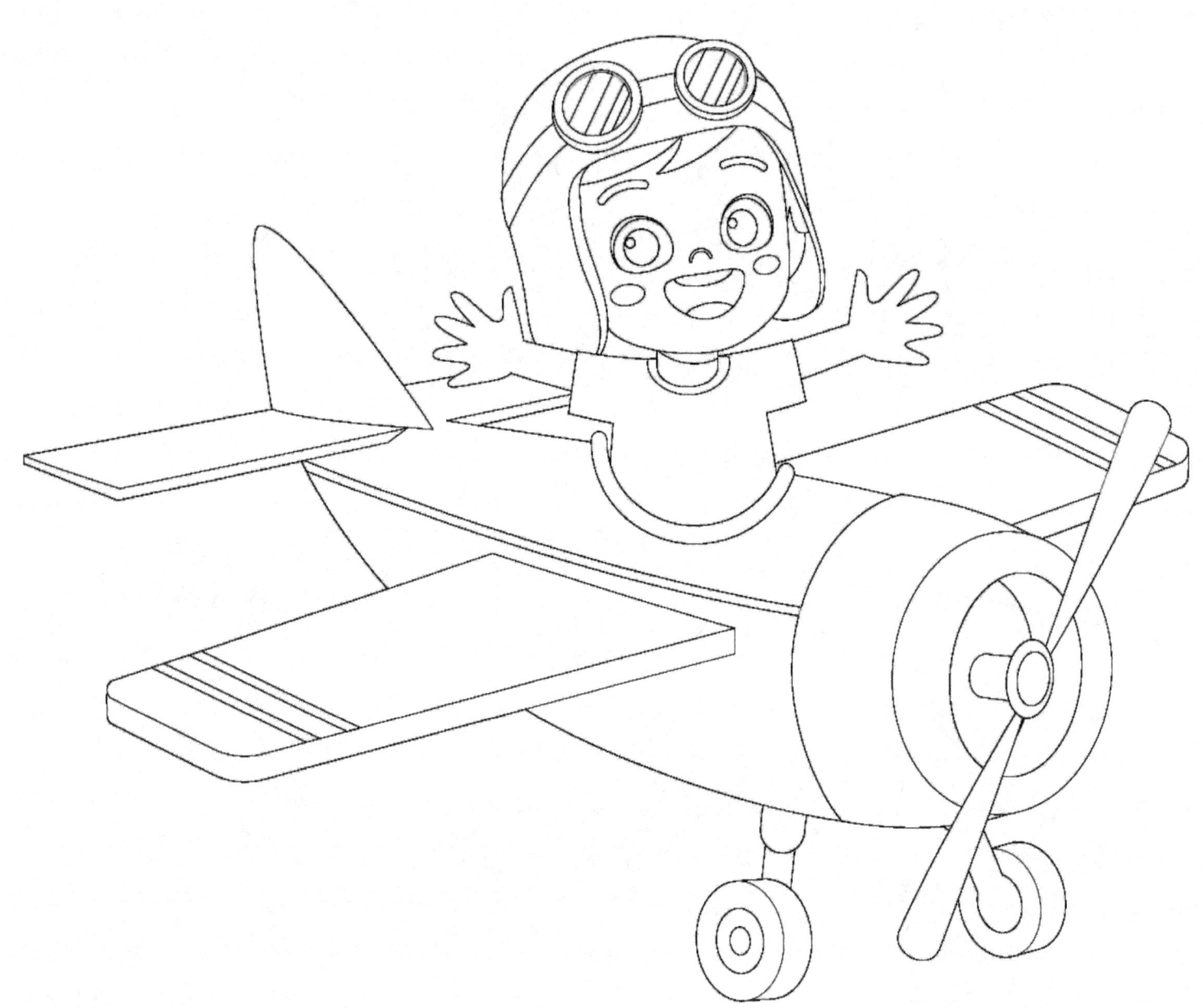

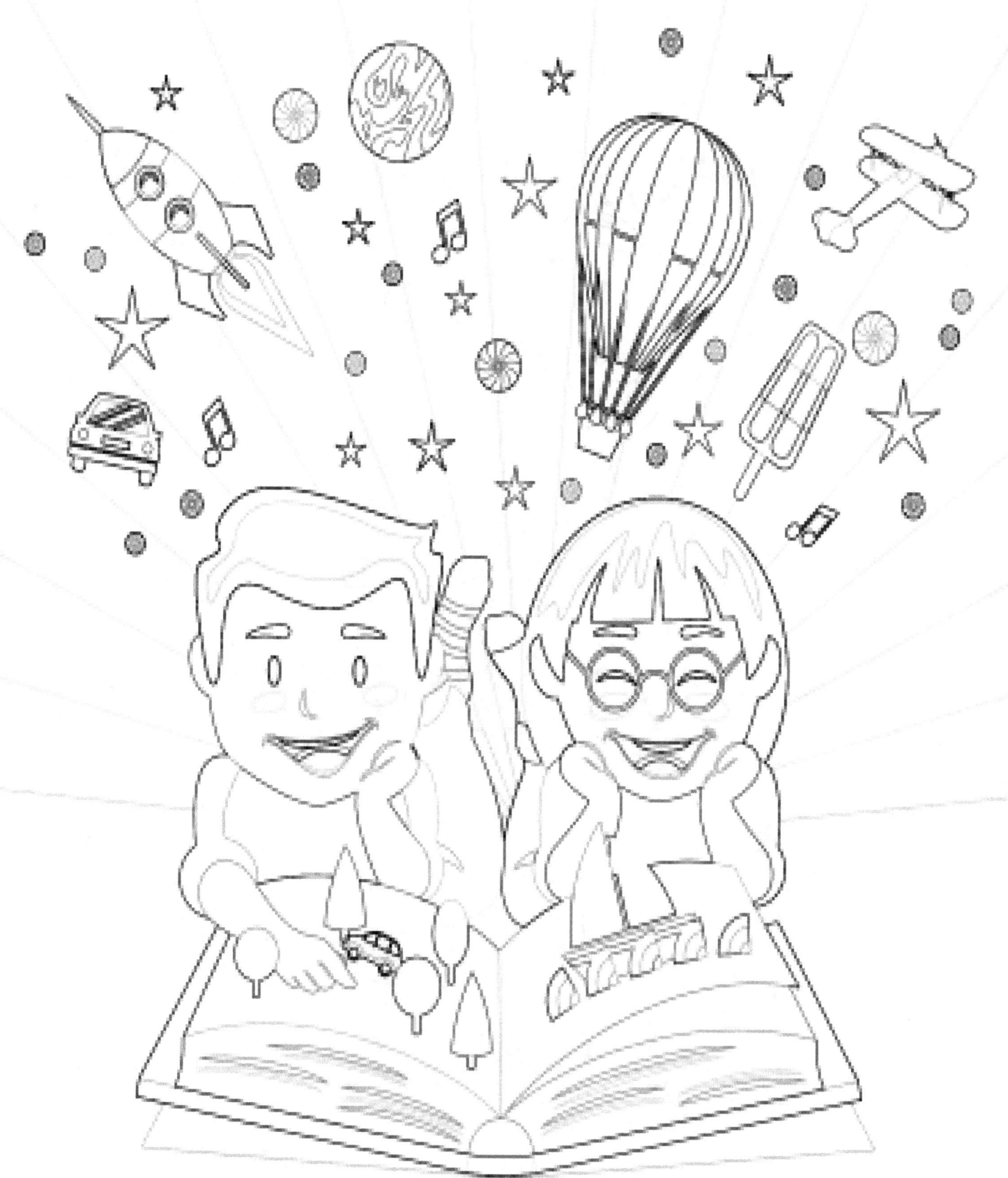

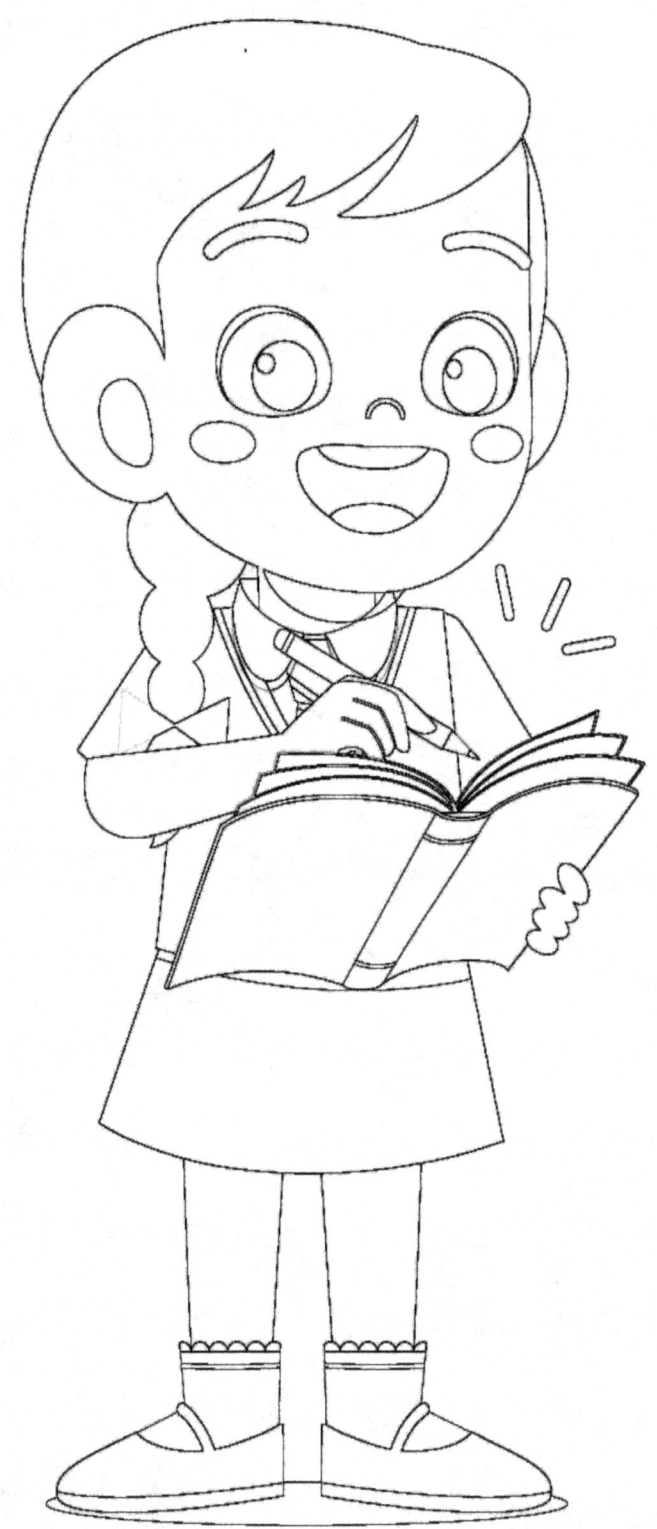

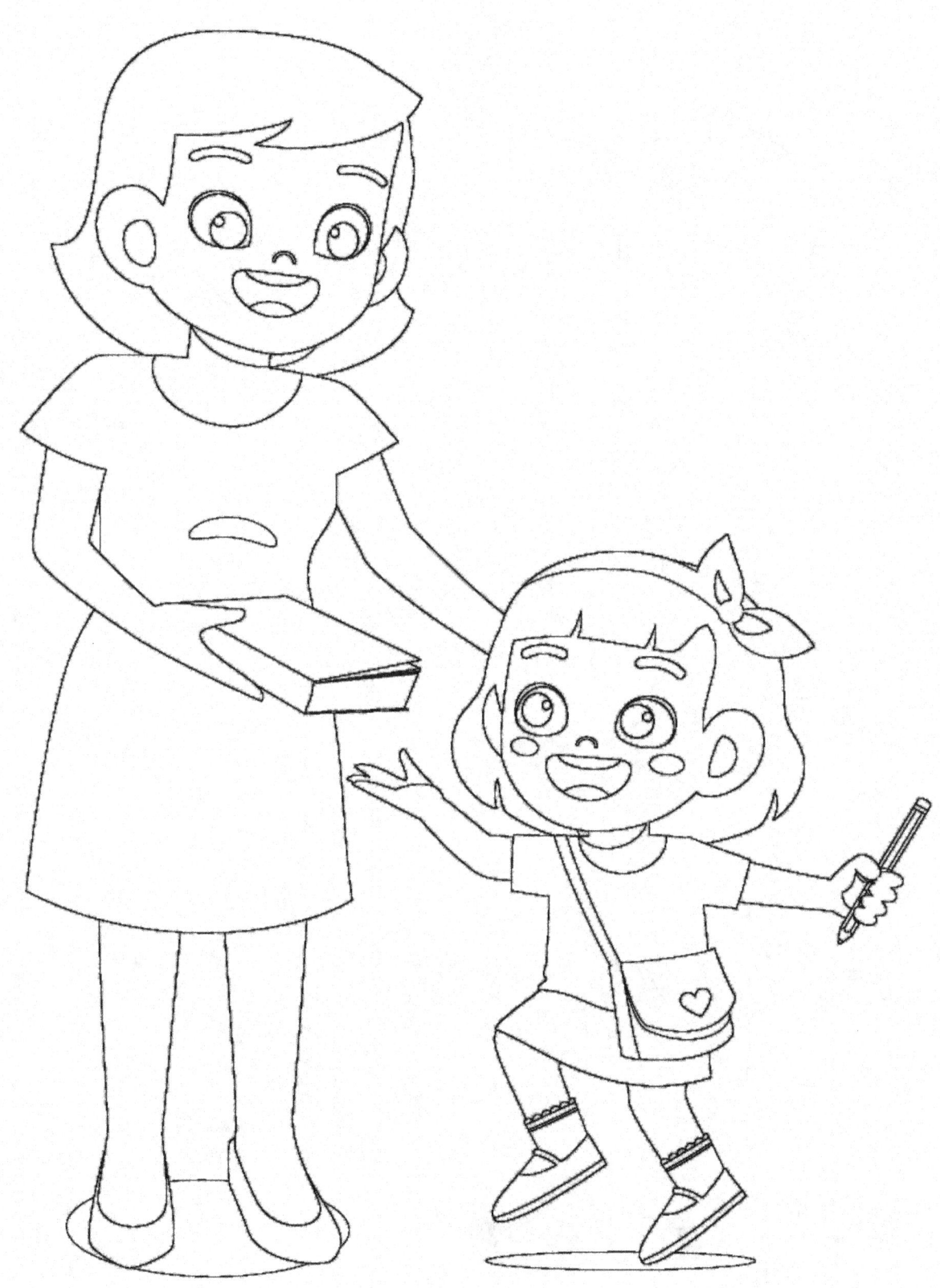

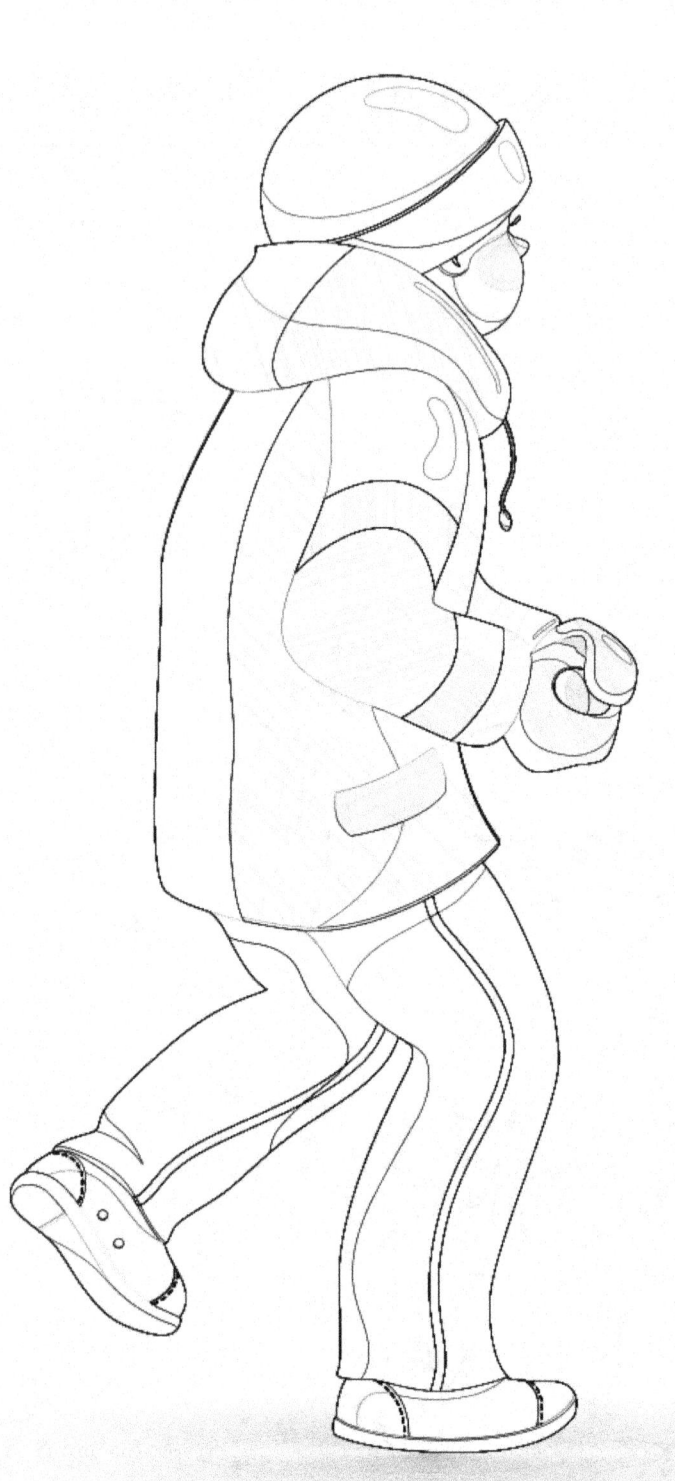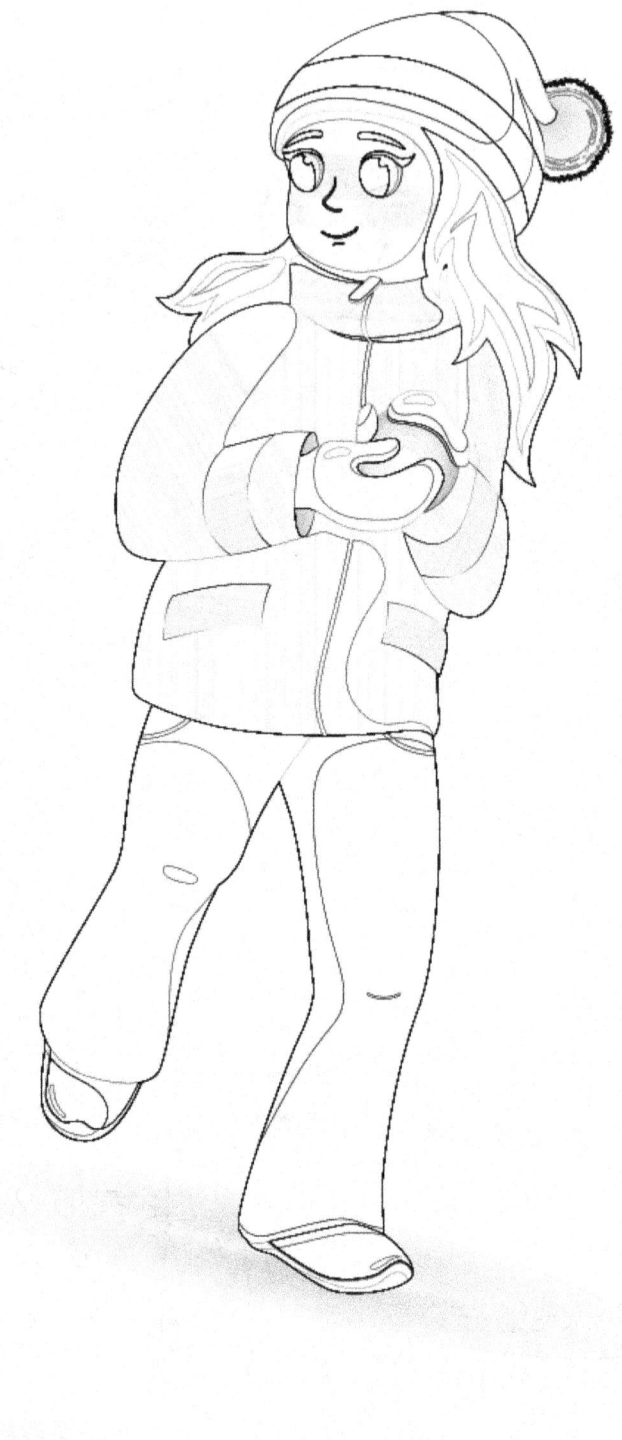

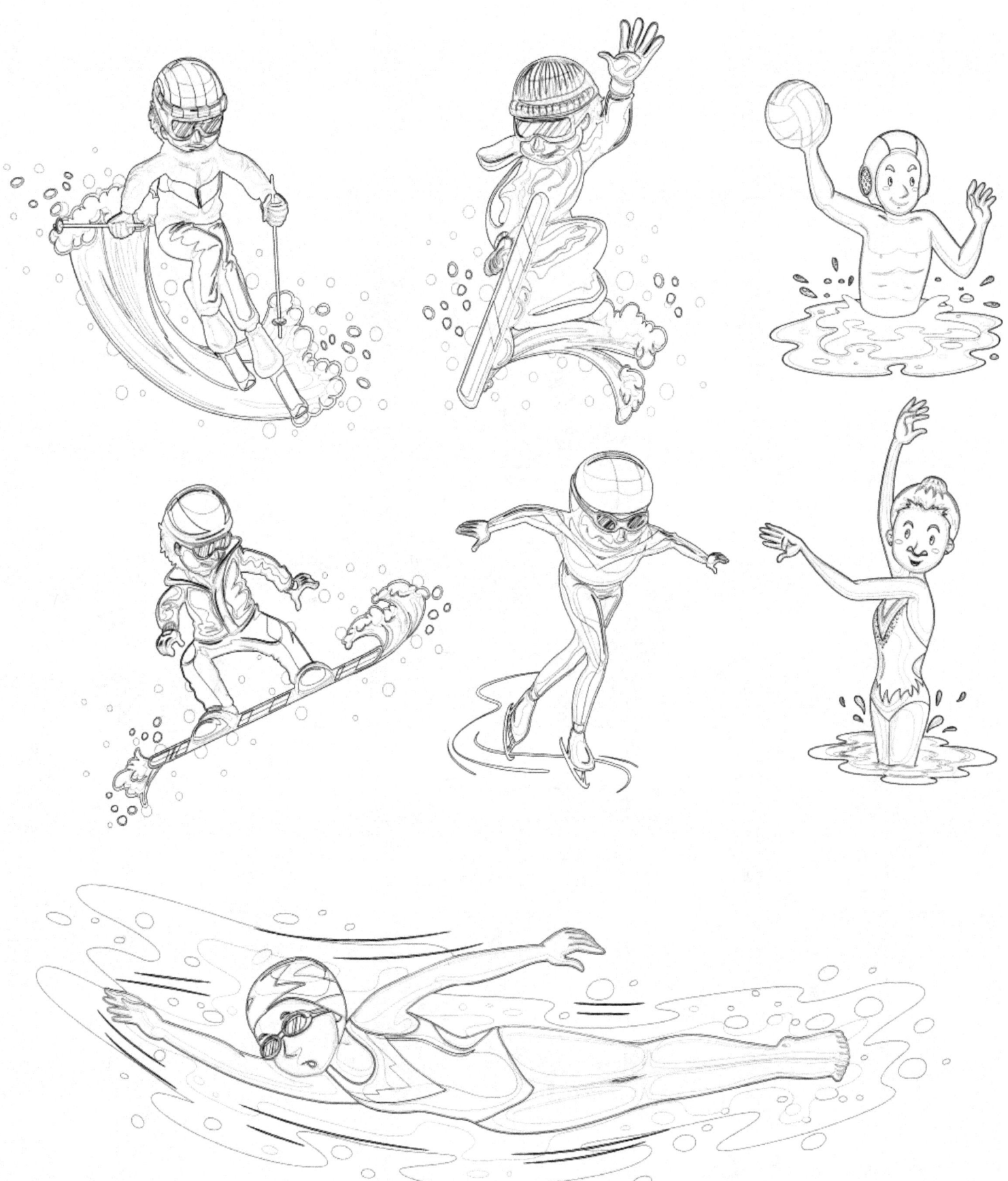

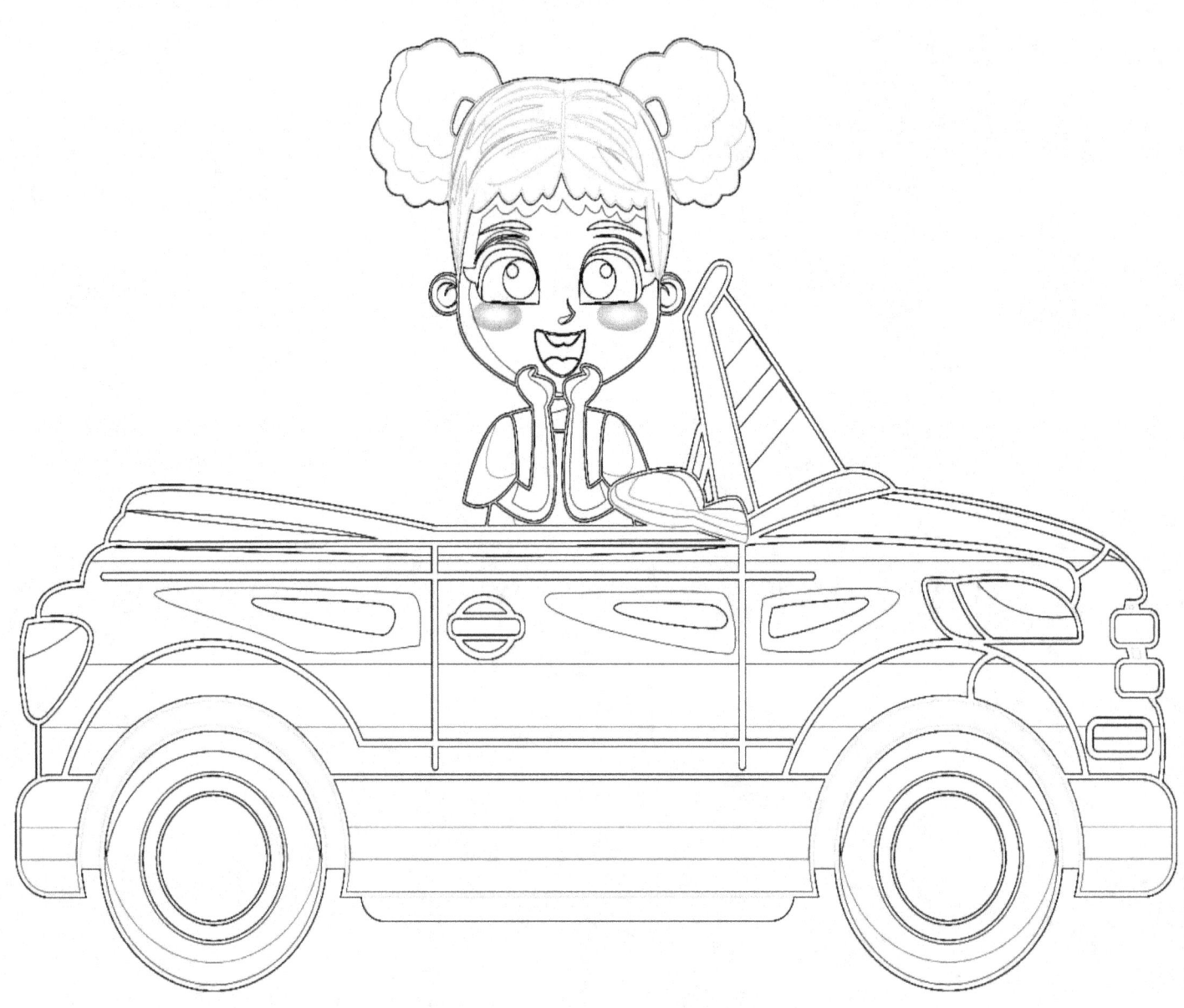

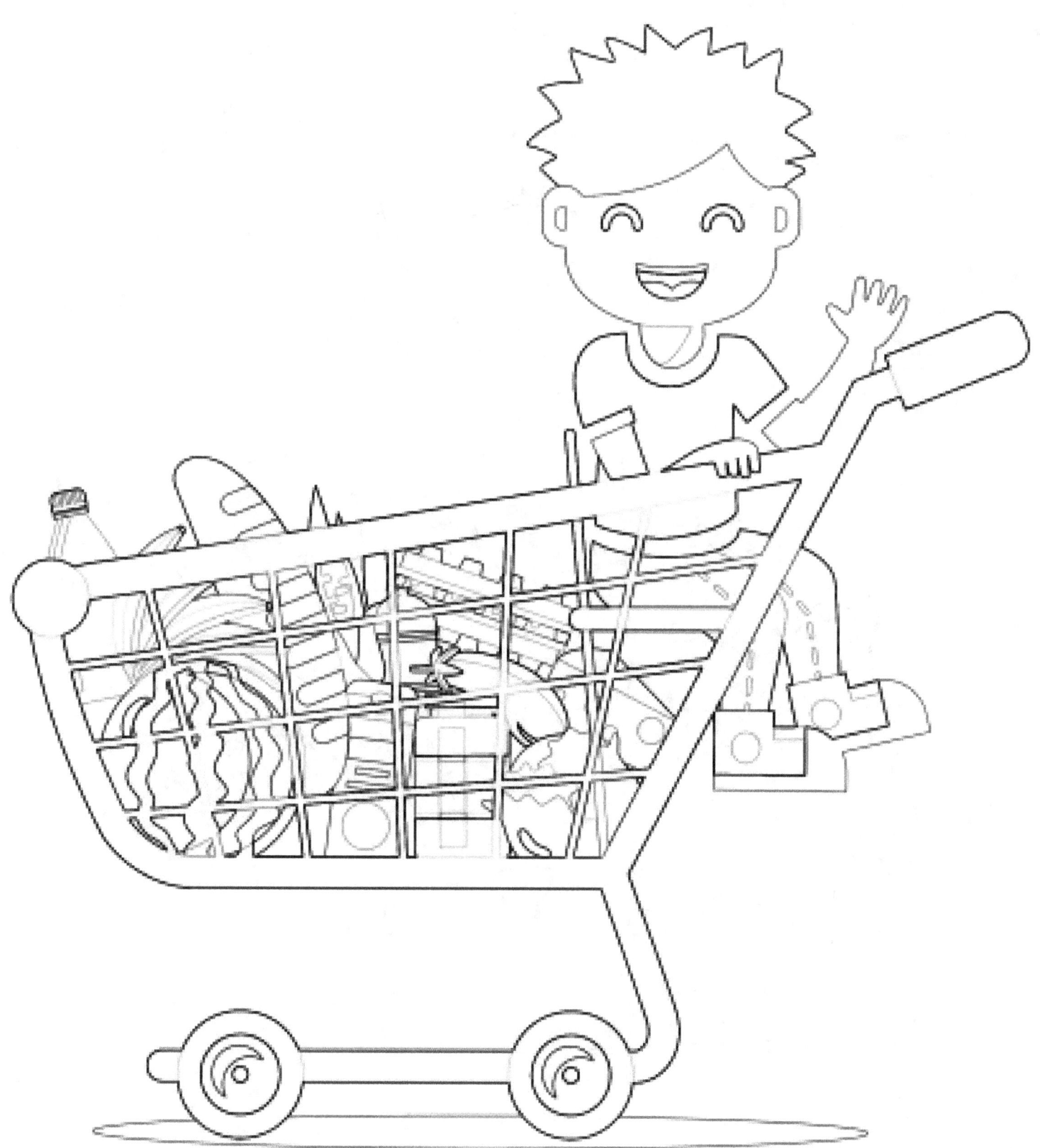

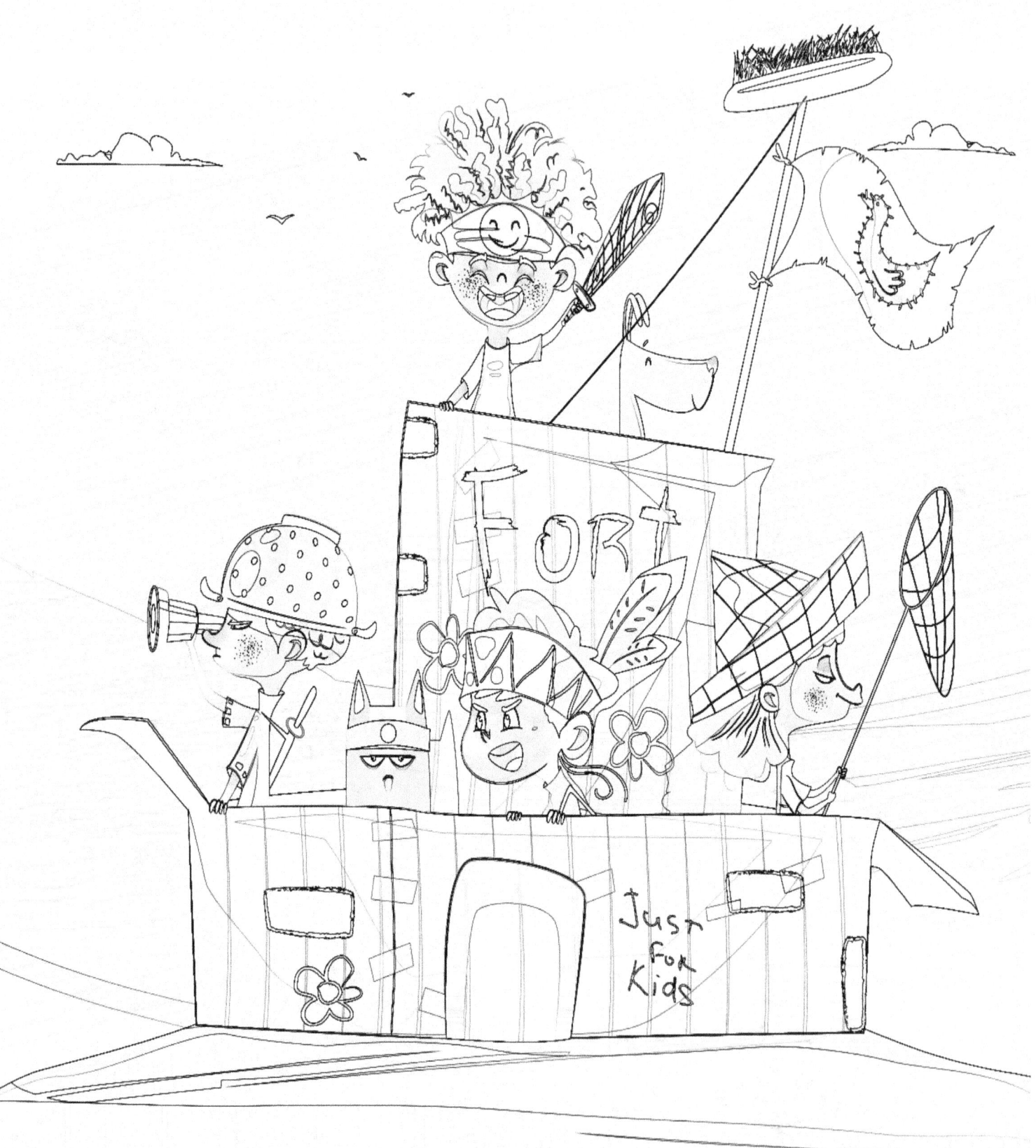

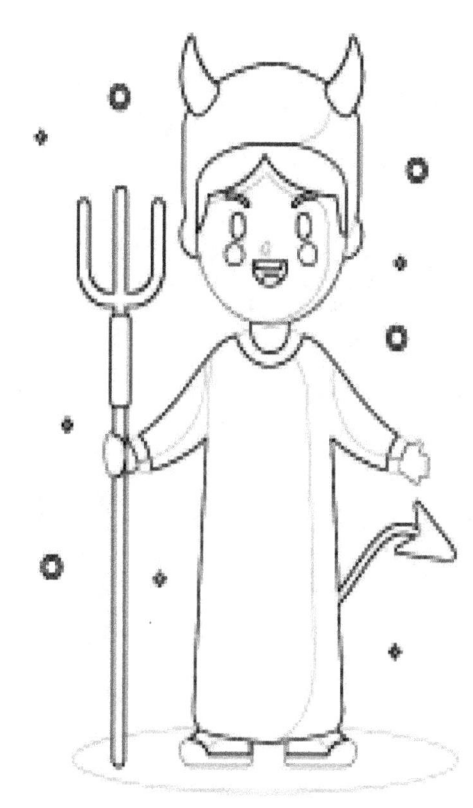
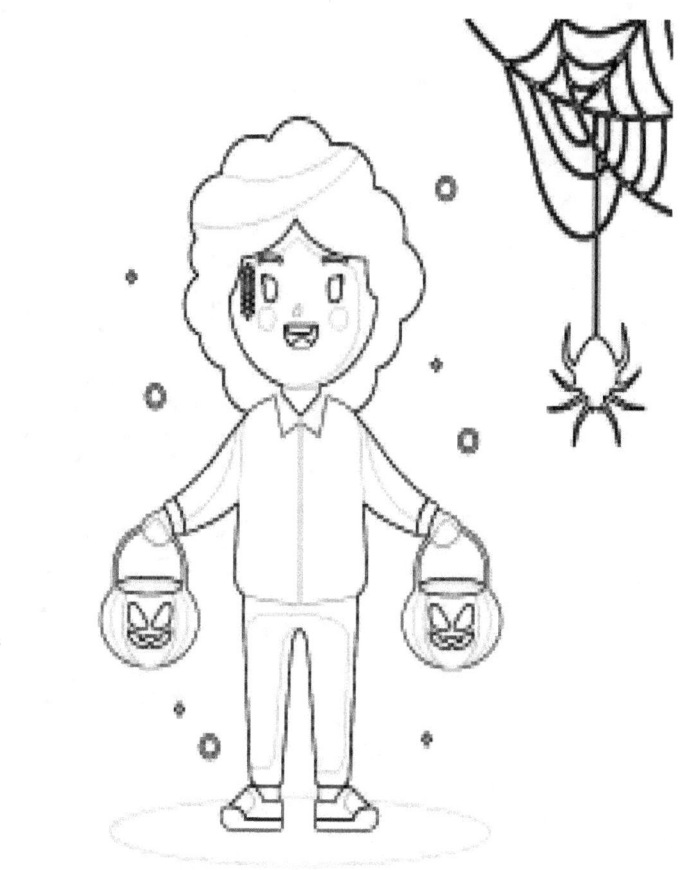
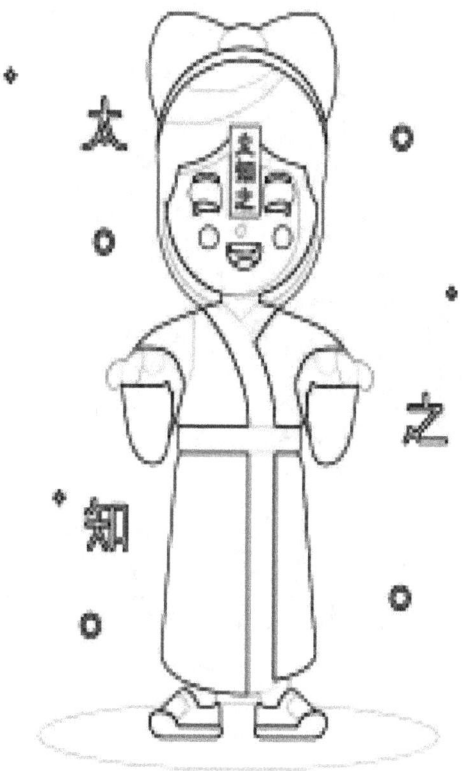
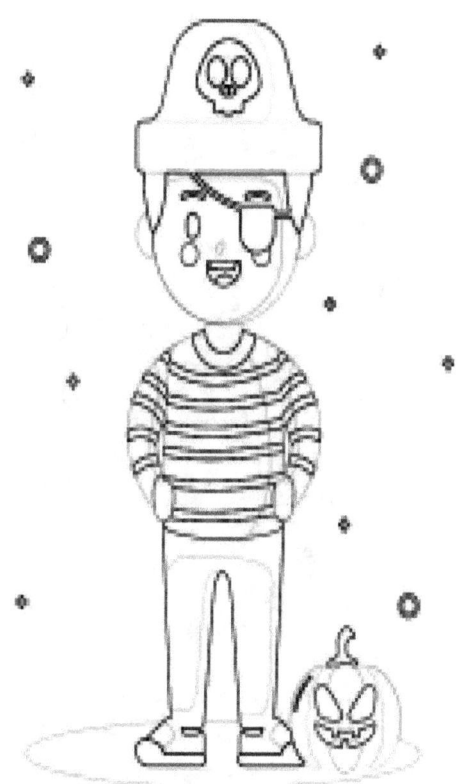

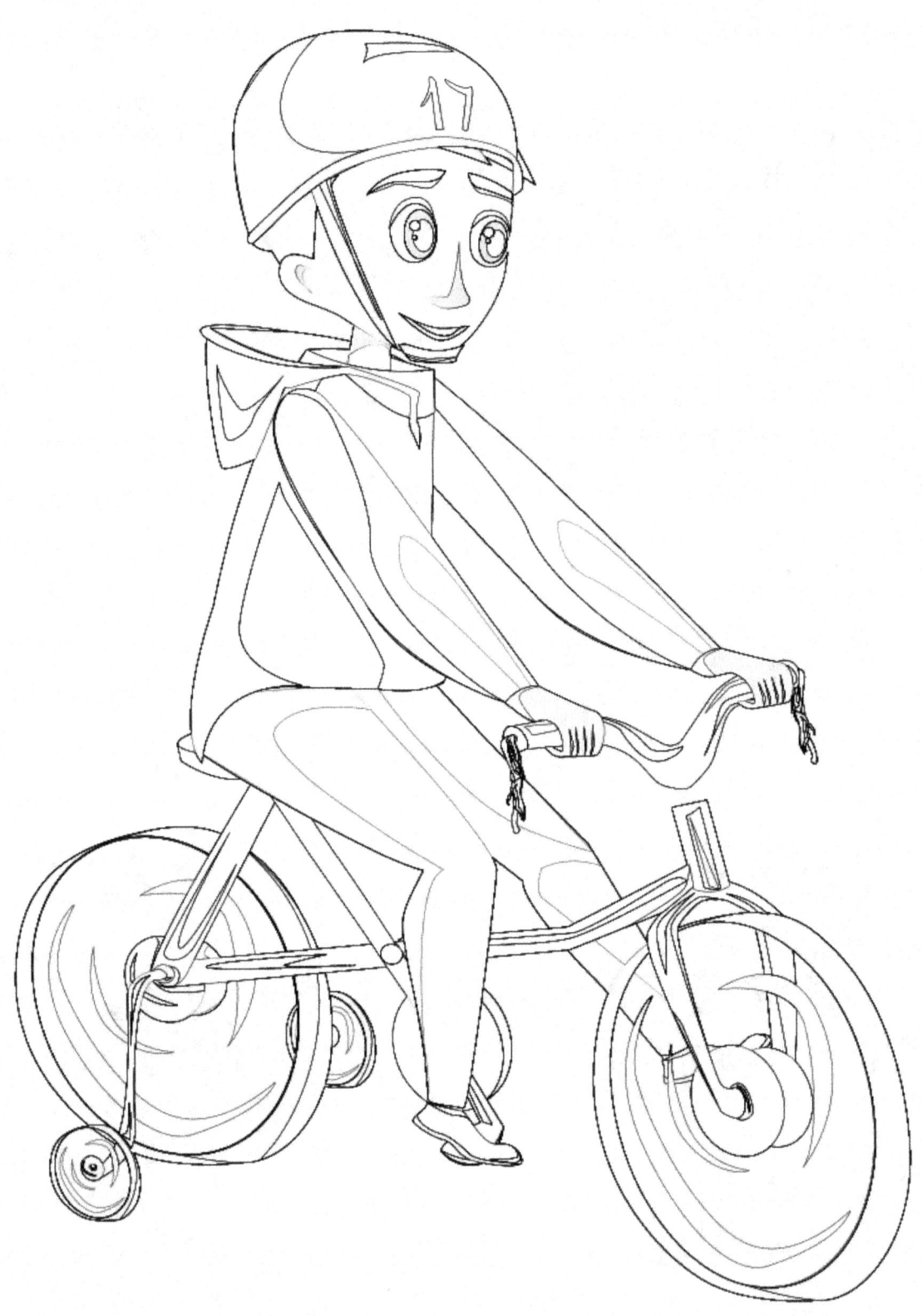

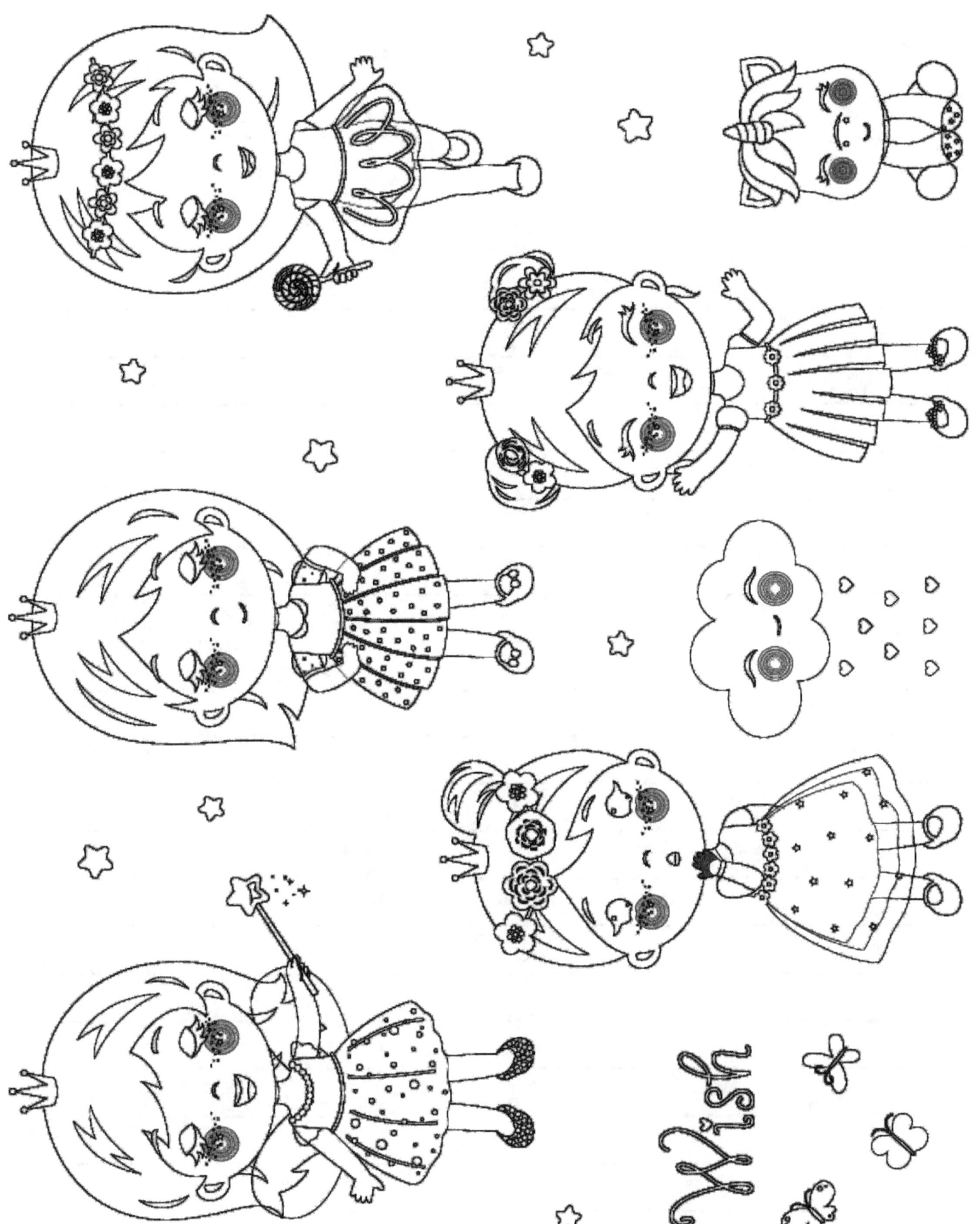

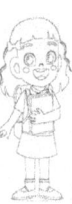

www.ingramcontent.com/pod-product-compliance
Lightning Source LLC
Chambersburg PA
CBHW081657220526
45466CB00009B/2787